SHAKESPEARE

ANTONY
AND CLEOPATRA

NOTES

COLES EDITORIAL BOARD

Bound to stay open

Publisher's Note

Otabind (Ota-bind). This book has been bound
using the patented Otabind process. You can
open this book at any page, gently run your
finger down the spine, and the pages will lie flat.

ABOUT COLES NOTES

COLES NOTES have been an indispensible aid to students on five continents since 1948.

COLES NOTES are available for a wide range of individual literary works. Clear, concise explanations and insights are provided along with interesting interpretations and evaluations.

Proper use of COLES NOTES will allow the student to pay greater attention to lectures and spend less time taking notes. This will result in a broader understanding of the work being studied and will free the student for increased participation in discussions.

COLES NOTES are an invaluable aid for review and exam preparation as well as an invitation to explore different interpretive paths.

COLES NOTES are written by experts in their fields. It should be noted that any literary judgement expressed herein is just that — the judgement of one school of thought. Interpretations that diverge from, or totally disagree with any criticism may be equally valid.

COLES NOTES are designed to supplement the text and are not intended as a substitute for reading the text itself. Use of the NOTES will serve not only to clarify the work being studied, but should enhance the reader's enjoyment of the topic.

ISBN 0-7740-3183-2

© COPYRIGHT 1991 AND PUBLISHED BY
COLES PUBLISHING COMPANY
TORONTO—CANADA
PRINTED IN CANADA

Manufactured by Webcom Limited
Cover finish: Webcom's Exclusive **Duracoat**

CONTENTS

Structure

Characters

Meaning

Style

Selected Criticisms

WILLIAM SHAKESPEARE
LIFE AND WORKS
Biographical Sketch

With the epithet "Dear Son of Memory", Milton praised Shakespeare as one constantly in our memories and brother of the Muses. Certainly no other author has held such sway over the literary world, undiminished through some three and a half centuries of shifting artistic tastes. Shakespeare's plots and his characters have continued to be a living reality for us; as his well known contemporary Ben Jonson wrote, in a familiar tribute, "Thou . . . art alive still, while thy Booke doth live,/ And we have wits to read, and praise to give."

The Early Years

Despite such acclaim and the scholarship it has spawned, our knowledge of Shakespeare's life is sketchy, filled with more questions than answers, even after we prune away the misinformation accumulated over the years. He was baptized on April 26, 1564, in Holy Trinity Church, Stratford-on-Avon. As it was customary to baptize children a few days after birth, we conjecture that he was born on April 23. The monument erected in Stratford states that he died on April 23, 1616, in his fifty-third year.

William was the third child of John Shakespeare, who came to Stratford from Snitterfield before 1532 as a "whyttawer" (tanner) and glover, and Mary Arden, daughter of a wealthy "gentleman of worship" from Wilmecote. They married around 1557. Since John Shakespeare owned one house on Greenhill Street and two on Henley Street, we cannot be certain where William was born, though the Henley Street shrine draws many tourists each year. William's two older sisters died in infancy, but three brothers and two other sisters survived at least into childhood.

Shakespeare's father was fairly well-to-do, dealing in farm products and wool, and owning considerable property in Stratford. After holding a series of minor municipal offices he was elected alderman in 1565, high bailiff (roughly similar to the mayor of today) in 1568, and chief alderman in 1571. There are no records of young Will Shakespeare's education (though there are many unfounded legends), but he undoubtedly attended the town school maintained by the burgesses, which prepared its students for the universities. Ben Jonson's line about Shakespeare's having "small *Latine*, and lesse *Greeke*" refers not to his education but to his lack of indebtedness to the classical writers and dramatists.

On November 27, 1582, a licence to marry was issued to "Willelmum Shaxpere *et* Annam Whateley *de* Temple Grafton," and on

1

the next day a marriage bond for "Willm Shagspere" and "Anne Hathwey of Stratford" was signed by Fulk Sandells and John Richardson, farmers of Stratford. This bond stated that there was no "lawful let or impediment by reason of any precontract, consanguinity, affinity, or by any other lawful means whatsoever"; thus "William and Anne (were) to be married together with once asking of the banns of matrimony." The problem of Anne Whateley has led many researchers and some detractors to argue all kinds of improbabilities, such as the existence of two different Shakespeares and the forging of documents to conceal Shakespeare's true identity. The actual explanation seems to be simple: the clerk who made the marriage licence entry apparently copied the name "Whateley" from a preceding entry, as a glance at the full sheet suggests. (Incidentally, Nicholas Rowe in his life of Shakespeare, published in 1709, well before the discovery of these marriage records, gave Anne's name as Hathaway.) The problems of marriage with Anne Hathaway — he was eighteen and she was twenty-six — and of the bond have caused similar consternation. Why did these two marry when there was such a discrepancy of age? Why only one saying of the banns (rather than the usual three)? Why the emphasis on a possible legal impediment? The answer here is not simple or definite, but the birth of a daughter Susanna, baptized at Holy Trinity on May 26, 1583, seems to explain the odd circumstances. It should be recognized, however, that an engagement to marry was considered legally binding in those days (we still have breach-of-promise suits today) and that premarital relations were not unusual or frowned upon when an engagement had taken place. The circumstances already mentioned, Shakespeare's ensuing activities, and his will bequeathing to Anne "my second best bed with the furniture" have suggested to some that their marriage was not entirely happy. Their other children, the twins Hamnet and Judith, were christened on February 2, 1585.

Theatrical Life

Shakespeare's years before and immediately after the time of his marriage are not charted, but rumor has him as an apprentice to a master butcher or as a country teacher or an actor with some provincial company. He is supposed to have run away from whatever he was doing for livelihood and to have gone to London, where he soon attached himself to some theatrical group. At this time there were only two professional houses established in the London environs, The Theatre (opened in 1576) and The Curtain (opened in 1577). His first connection with the theater was reputedly as holder of horses; that is, one of the stage crew, but a most inferior assignment. Thereafter he became an actor (perhaps at this time he met Ben Jonson), a writer, and a director. Such experience had its mark in the theatricality of his plays. We do know that he was established in London by 1592, when Robert Greene lamented in *A Groatsworth of Wit* (September, 1592) that professional actors had gained priority in the theater over university-trained writers like himself: "There is an upstart Crow, beautified with our feathers, that with his *Tygers hart wrapt in a Players hyde*, supposes he is as well able to bombast out a lanke verse as the best of you: and beeing an absolute *Iohannes fac totum* (Jack-of-all-trades), is in his owne conceit the onely Shake-scene in a countrey." An apology for Greene's ill-humored statement by Henry Chettle, the editor of the pamphlet, appeared around December 1592 in *Kind-Hart's Dream*.

Family Affairs

To return to the known details of family life, Shakespeare's son Hamnet was buried at Stratford on August 11, 1596; his father was given a coat of arms on October 20, 1596; and he purchased New Place (a refurbished tourist attraction today) on May 4, 1597. The London playwright obviously had not severed connections with his birthplace, and he was reflecting his new affluence by being known as William Shakespeare of Stratford-upon-Avon, in the County of Warwick, Gentleman. His father was buried in Stratford on September 8, 1601; his mother, on September 9, 1608. His daughter Susanna married Dr. John Hall on June 5, 1607, and they had a child named Elizabeth. His other daughter, Judith, married Thomas Quiney on February 10, 1616, without special licence, during Lent and was thus excommunicated. Shakespeare revised his will on March 25, 1616, and was buried on April 25, 1616 (according to the parish register). A monument by Gerard Janssen was erected in the Holy Trinity chancel in 1623 but many, like Milton several years later, protested:

> What needs my *Shakespeare* for his honour'd Bones,
> The labour of an age in piled Stone, . . .
> Thou in our wonder and astonishment
> Hast built thy self a live-long Monument.

Shakespeare's Writings

Order of Appearance

Dating of Shakespeare's early plays, while based on inconclusive evidence, has tended to hover around the early 1590's. Almost certainly it is his chronicles of Henry the Sixth that Philip Henslowe, an important theatrical manager of the day, referred to in his diary as being performed during March-May, 1592. An allusion to these plays also occurs in Thomas Nashe's *Piers Penniless His Supplication to the Devil* (August, 1592). Greene's quotation about a tiger is a paraphrase of "O tiger's heart wrapt in a woman's hide" from *Henry VI*, Part III.

The first published work to come from Shakespeare's hand was *Venus and Adonis* (1593), a long stanzaic poem, dedicated to Henry

Wriothesley, Earl of Southampton. A year later *The Rape of Lucrece* appeared, also dedicated to Southampton. Perhaps poetry was pursued during these years because the London theaters were closed as a result of a virulent siege of plague. The *Sonnets*, published in 1609, may owe something to Southampton, who had become Shakespeare's patron. Perhaps some were written as early as the first few years of the 1590's. They were mentioned (along with a number of plays) in 1598 by Francis Meres in his *Palladis Tamia*, and sonnets 138 and 144 were printed without authority by William Jaggard in *The Passionate Pilgrim* (1599).

There is a record of a performance of *A Comedy of Errors* at Gray's Inn (one of the law colleges) on December 28, 1594, and, during early 1595, Shakespeare was paid, along with the famous actors Richard Burbage and William Kempe, for performances before the Queen by the Lord Chamberlain's Men, a theatrical company formed the year before. The company founded the Globe Theatre on the south side of the Thames in 1599 and became the King's Men when James ascended the throne. Records show frequent payments to the company through its general manager John Heminge. From 1595 through 1614 there are numerous references to real estate transactions and other legal matters, to many performances, and to various publications connected with Shakespeare.

Order of Publication

The first plays to be printed were *Titus Andronicus* around February, 1594, and the garbled versions of *Henry VI*, Parts II and III in 1594. (Some scholars, however, question whether the last two are versions of *Henry VI*, Parts II and III, and some dispute Shakespeare's authorship.) Thereafter *Richard III* appeared in 1597 and 1598; *Richard II*, in 1597 and twice in 1598; *Romeo and Juliet*, in 1597 (a pirated edition) and 1599, and many others. Some of the plays appear in individual editions, with or without Shakespeare's name on the title page, but eighteen are known only from their appearance in the first collected volume (the so-called First Folio) of 1623. The editors were Heminge and Henry Condell, another member of Shakespeare's company. *Pericles* was omitted from the First Folio although it had appeared in 1609, 1611, and 1619; it was added to the Third Folio in 1664.

There was reluctance to publish plays at this time for various reasons; many plays were carelessly written for fast production; collaboration was frequent; plays were not really considered *reading* matter; they were sometimes circulated in manuscript; and the theatrical company, not the author, owned the rights. Those plays given individual publication appeared in a quarto, so named from the size of the page. A single sheet of paper was folded twice to make four leaves (thus *quarto*) or eight pages; these four leaves constitute one signature (one section of a bound book). A page measures about 6¾ in. x 8½ in. On the other hand, a folio sheet is folded once to make two leaves or four pages; three sheets, or twelve pages, constitute a signature. The page is approximately 8½ in. x 13⅜ in.

Authorized publication occurred when a company disbanded, when money was needed but rights were to be retained, when a play failed or ran into licensing difficulties (thus, hopefully, the printed work would justify the play against the criticism), or when a play had been pirated. Authorized editions are called good quartos. Piratical publication might occur when the manuscript of a play had circulated privately, when a member of a company desired money for himself, or when a stenographer or memorizer took the play down in the theater (such a version was recognizable by inclusion of stage directions derived from an eyewitness, by garbled sections, etc.). Pirated editions are called bad quartos; there are at least five bad quartos of Shakespeare's plays.

Authenticity of Works

Usually thirty-seven plays are printed in modern collections of Shakespeare's works but some recent scholars have urged the addition of two more: *Edward III* and *Two Noble Kinsmen*. A case has also been advanced, unconvincingly, for a fragment of the play on Sir Thomas More. At times, six of the generally-accepted plays have been questioned: *Henry VI*, Parts I, II and III, *Timon of Athens*, *Pericles* and *Henry VIII*. The first four are usually accepted today (one hopes all question concerning *Timon* has finally ended), but if Shakespeare did not write these plays in their entirety, he certainly wrote parts of them. Of course, collaboration in those days was commonplace. Aside from the two long narrative poems already mentioned and the sonnets (Nos. 1-152, but not Nos. 153-154), Shakespeare's poetic output is uncertain. *The Passionate Pilgrim* (1599) contains only five authenticated poems (two sonnets and three verses from *Love's Labour's Lost*); *The Phoenix and the Turtle* (1601) may be his, but the authenticity of *A Lover's Complaint* (appended to the sonnets) is highly questionable.

Who Was Shakespeare?

At this point we might mention a problem that has plagued Shakespeare study for over a century: who was Shakespeare? Those who would like to make the author of the plays someone else — Francis Bacon or the Earl of Oxford or even Christopher Marlowe (dead long before most of the plays were written) — have used the lack of information of Shakespeare's early years and the confusion in the evidence we have been examining to advance their candidate. But the major arguments against Shakespeare show the source of these speculators' disbelief to be in classconscious snobbery and perhaps in a perverse adherence to minority opinion. The most common argument is that no one of Shakespeare's background, lack of education, and lack of aristocratic experience could know all that the author knew. But study will reveal that such information was readily available in various popular sources, that some of it lies in the literary sources used for the play, and that Shakespeare was probably not totally lacking in education or in social decorum. The more significant question of style and tone is not dealt with — nor could it successfully be raised. Bacon, for example, no matter how much we admire his mind and his writings, exhibits a writing style diametrically opposite to Shakespeare's, a style most unpoetic and often flat. The student would be wise not to waste time rehashing these unfounded theories. No such question was raised in the seventeenth or eighteenth centuries, and no serious student of the plays today doubts that Shakespeare *was* Shakespeare.

Shakespeare's Plays

Exact dates for Shakespeare's plays remain a source of debate among scholars. The following serve only as a general frame of reference.

	COMEDIES	TRAGEDIES	HISTORIES
1591			Henry VI, Part I
1592	Comedy of Errors		Henry VI, Part II
1592	Two Gentlemen of Verona		Henry VI, Part III
1593	Love's Labour's Lost	Titus Andronicus	Richard III
1594			King John
1595	Midsummer Night's Dream	Romeo and Juliet	Richard II
1596	Merchant of Venice		
1596	Taming of the Shrew		
1597			Henry IV, Part I
1598	Much Ado About Nothing		Henry IV, Part II
1599	As You Like It	Julius Caesar	
1599	Merry Wives of Windsor		Henry V
1601	Twelfth Night	Hamlet	
1602	Troilus and Cressida		
1602	All's Well That Ends Well		
1604	Measure for Measure	Othello	
1605		King Lear	
1606		Macbeth	
1607		Timon of Athens	
1607		Antony and Cleopatra	
1608	Pericles		
1609		Coriolanus	
1610	Cymbeline		
1611	Winter's Tale		
1611	Tempest		
1613			Henry VIII

Shakespeare's England

The world of Elizabethan and Jacobean England was a world of growth and change. The great increase in the middle class, and in the population as a whole, demanded a new economy and means of livelihood, a new instrument of government (one recognizing "rights" and changed class structure), a new social code and a broad base of entertainment. The invention of printing a century before had contributed to that broader base, but it was the theater that supplied the more immediate needs of the greatest numbers. The theater grew and along with it came less-educated, more money-conscious writers, who gave the people what they wanted: entertainment. But Shakespeare, having passed through a brief period of hack writing, proceeded to set down important ideas in memorable language throughout most of his career. His plays, particularly the later ones, have been analyzed by recent critics in terms of literary quality through their metaphor, verse-line, relationships with psychology and myth, and elaborate structure. Yet Shakespeare was a man of the stage, and the plays were written to be performed. Only this will fully account for the humor of a deadly serious play like *Hamlet* or the spectacle of a *Coriolanus*.

Life in London

During Shakespeare's early years there, London was a walled city of about 200,000, with seven gates providing access to the city from the east, north, and west. It was geographically small and crisscrossed by narrow little streets and lanes. The various wards each had a parish church that dominated the life of the close-knit community. To the south and outside were slums and the haunts of criminal types, and farther out were the agricultural lands and huge estates. As the population increased and the central area declined, the fashionable people of the city moved toward the west, where the palace of Westminster lay. Houses were generally rented out floor by floor and sometimes room by room. Slums were common within the city, too, though close to pleasant enough streets and squares. "Merrie Olde England" was not really clean, nor were its people, for in those days there were no sewers or drains except the gutter in the middle of the street, into which garbage would be emptied to be floated off by the rain to Fleet ditch or Moor ditch. Plague was particularly ravaging in 1592, 1593-94 (when the theaters were closed to avoid contamination) and 1603. Medical knowledge, of course, was slight; ills were "cured" by amputation, leeching, blood-letting and cathartics. The city was (and still is) dominated by St. Paul's Cathedral, around which booksellers clustered on Paternoster Row.

Religious Atmosphere

Of great significance for the times was religion. Under Elizabeth, a state church had developed; it was Protestant in nature and was called Anglican (or today, Episcopalian) but it had arisen from Henry VIII's break with the Pope and from a compromise with the Roman Catholics who had gained power under Mary Tudor.

The Church of England was headed by the Archbishop of Canter bury, who was to be an increasingly important figure in the early part of the seventeenth century. There were also many schismatic groups, which generally desired further departures from Roman Catholicism. Calvinists were perhaps the most numerous and important of the Protestant groups. The Puritans, who were Calvinist, desired to "purify" the church of ritual and certain dogmas, but during the 1590's they were lampooned as extremists in dress and conduct.

Political Milieu

During Shakespeare's lifetime there were two monarchs: Elizabeth, 1558-1603, and James I, 1603-1625. Elizabeth was the daughter of Henry VIII and Anne Boleyn, his second wife, who was executed in 1536. After Henry's death, his son by his third wife, Jane Seymore (died in 1537), reigned as Edward VI. He was followed by Mary Tudor, daughter of Henry's first wife, Catherine of Aragon. Mary was a Roman Catholic, who tried to put down religious dissension by persecution of both Protestants and Catholics. Nor did her marriage to Philip II of Spain endear her to the people.

Elizabeth's reign was troubled by many offers of marriage, particularly from Spanish and French nobles — all Roman Catholic — and by the people's concern for an heir to the throne. English suitors generally cancelled one another out by intrigue or aggressiveness. One of the most prominent was the Earl of Essex, Robert Devereux, who fell in and out of favor; he apparently attempted to take over the reins of control, only to be captured, imprisoned and executed in February, 1601. One claimant to the throne was Mary of Scotland, a Roman Catholic and widow of Francis II of France. She was the second cousin of Elizabeth, tracing her claim through her grandmother, who was Henry VIII's sister. Finally, settlement came with Elizabeth's acceptance of Mary's son as heir apparent, though Mary was to be captured, tried and executed for treason in 1587. Mary had abdicated the throne of Scotland in 1567 in favor of her son, James VI. His ascent to the throne of England in 1603 as James I joined the two kingdoms for the first time, although Scotland during the seventeenth century often acted independently of England.

Contemporary Events

Political and religious problems were intermingled in the celebrated Gunpowder Plot. Angry over fines that were levied upon those not attending Church of England services — primarily Roman Catholics — and offended by difficulties over papal envoys, a group of Catholics plotted to blow up Parliament, and James with it, at its first session on November 5, 1605. A cache of gunpowder was stored in the cellar, guarded by various conspirators, among them Guy Fawkes. The plot was discovered before it could be carried out and Fawkes, on duty at the time, was apprehended. The execution of the plotters and the triumph of the anti-Papists led in succeeding years to celebrations in the streets and the hanging of Fawkes in effigy.

Among the most noteworthy public events during these times were the wars with the Spanish, which included the defeat of the Spanish Armada in 1588, the battle in the Lowlands in 1590-1594, the expedition to Cadiz under Essex in 1596 and the expedition to the Azores (the Islands Expedition), also under Essex, in 1597. With trading companies especially set up for colonization and exploitation, travel excited the imagination of the people: here was a new way of life, here were new customs brought back by the sailors and merchants, here was a new dream world to explore.

In all, the years from around 1590 to 1601 were trying ones for English people, relieved only by the news from abroad, the new affluence and the hope for the future under James. Writers of the period frequently reflect, however, the disillusionment and sadness of those difficult times.

The Elizabethan Theater

Appearance

The Elizabethan playhouse developed from the medieval inn with its rooms grouped around a courtyard into which a stage was built. This pattern was used in The Theatre, built by James Burbage in 1576: a square frame building (later round or octagonal) with a square yard, three tiers of galleries, each jutting out over the one below, and a stage extending into the middle of the yard, where people stood or sat on improvised seats. There was no cover over the yard or stage and lighting was therefore natural. Thus performances were what we might consider late matinees or early evening performances; in summer, daylight continues in London until around ten o'clock.

Other theaters were constructed during the ensuing years: The Curtain in 1577, The Rose in 1587 (on Bankside), The Swan in 1595 (also Bankside) and Shakespeare's playhouse, The Globe, in 1599 (not far from The Rose). There is still some question about the exact dimensions of this house, but it seems to have been octagonal, each side measuring about 36 feet, with an over-all diameter of 84 feet. It was about 33 feet to the eaves, and the yard was 56 feet in diameter. Three sides were used for backstage and to serve the needs of the players. There was no curtain or proscenium, hence the spectators became part of the action. Obviously, the actors' asides and soliloquies were effective under these conditions.

There was no real scenery and there were only a few major props; thus the lines of the play had to reveal locations and movement, changes in time or place, etc. In this way, too, it was easier to establish a nonrealistic setting, for all settings were created in words. On either side of the stage were doors, within the flooring were trapdoors (for

9

entrances of ghosts, etc.), and behind the main stage was the inner stage or recess. Here, indoor scenes (such as a court or a bedchamber) were played, and some props could be used because the inner stage was usually concealed by a curtain when not in use. It might also have served to hide someone behind the ever-present arras, like Polonius in *Hamlet*. The "chamber" was on the second level, with windows and a balcony. On the third level was another chamber, primarily for musicians.

Actors

An acting company such as the Lord Chamberlain's Men was a fellowship of ten to fifteen sharers with some ten to twelve extras, three or four boys (often to play women's roles) who might become full sharers, and stagehands. There were rival companies, each with its leading dramatist and leading tragic actor and clown. The Lord Admiral's Men, organized in 1594, boasted Ben Jonson and the trage-dian Edward Alleyn. Some of the rivalry of this War of the Theaters is reflected in the speeches of Hamlet, who also comments on the ascendancy and unwarranted popularity of the children's companies (like the Children of Blackfriars) in the late 1590's.

The company dramatist, of course, had to think in terms of the members of his company as he wrote his play. He had to make use of the physical features and peculiar talents of the actors, making sure, besides, that there was a role for each member. The fact that women's parts were taken by boys imposed obvious limitations on the range of action. Accordingly, we often find women characters impersonating men; for example, Robert Goffe played Portia in *The Merchant of Venice*, and Portia impersonates a male lawyer in the important trial scene. Goffe also played Juliet, and Anne in *Richard III*, and Oberon in *Midsummer Night's Dream*. The influence of an actor on the playwright can be seen, on the one hand, by noting the "humor" characters portrayed so competently by Thomas Pope, who was a choleric Mercutio in *Romeo*, a melancholic Jaques in *As You Like It*, and a sanguinary Falstaff in *Henry IV*, Part I; and by comparing, on the other hand, the clown Bottom in *Midsummer Night's Dream*, played in a frolicsome manner by William Kempe, with the clown Feste in *Twelfth Night*, sung and danced by Robert Armin. Obviously, too, if a certain kind of character was not available within the company, then that kind of character could not be written into the play. The approach was decidedly different from ours today, where the play almost always comes first and the casting of roles second. The plays were performed in a repertory system, with a different play each afternoon. The average life of a play was about ten performances.

History of the Drama

English drama goes back to native forms developed from playlets presented at Church holidays. Mystery plays dealt with biblical stories

10

such as the Nativity or the Passion, and miracle plays usually depicted the lives of saints. The merchant and craft guilds that came to own and produce the cycles of plays were the forerunners of the theatrical companies of Shakespeare's time. The kind of production these cycles received, either as moving pageants in the streets or as staged shows in a churchyard, influenced the late sixteenth-century production of a secular play: there was an intimacy with the audience and there was a great reliance on words rather than setting and props. Similar involvement with the stage action is experienced by audiences of the arena theater of today.

The morality play, the next form to develop, was an allegory of the spiritual conflict between good and evil in the soul of man. The *dramatis personae* were abstract virtues and vices, with at least one man representing Mankind (or Everyman, as the most popular of these plays was titled). Some modern critics see *Othello* as a kind of morality play in which the soul of Othello is vied for by the aggressively evil Iago (as a kind of Satanic figure) and passively good Desdemona (as a personification of Christian faith in all men). The Tudor interlude — a short, witty, visual play — may have influenced the subplot of the Elizabethan play with its low-life and jesting and visual tricks. In mid-sixteenth century appeared the earliest known English comedies, Nicholas Udall's *Ralph Roister Doister* and *Gammer Gurton's Needle* (of uncertain authorship). Both show the influence of the Roman comic playwright Plautus. Shakespeare's *Comedy of Errors*, performed in the 1590's, was an adaptation of Plautus' *Menaechmi*, both plays featuring twins and an involved story of confused identities. The influence of the Roman tragedian Seneca can be traced from Thomas Norton and Thomas Sackville in *Gorboduc* to *Hamlet*. Senecan tragedy is a tragedy of revenge, characterized by many deaths, much blood-letting, ghosts, feigned madness and the motif of a death for a death.

Shakespeare's Artistry

Plots

Generally, a Shakespearean play has two plots: a main plot and a subplot. The subplot reflects the main plot and is often concerned with inferior characters. Two contrasting examples will suffice: Lear and his daughters furnish the characters for the main plot of filial love and ingratitude, whereas Gloucester and his sons enact the same theme in the subplot; Lear and Gloucester both learn that outward signs of love may be false. In *Midsummer Night's Dream*, the town workmen (Quince, Bottom *et al*.) put on a tragic play in such a hilarious way that it turns the subject of the play — love so strong that the hero will kill himself if his loved one dies first — into farce, but this in the main plot is the "serious" plight of the four mixed-up lovers. In both examples Shakespeare has reinforced his points by subplots dealing with the same subject as the main plot.

Sources

The plots of the Elizabethan plays were usually adapted from other sources. "Originality" was not the sought quality; a kind of variation on a theme was. It was felt that one could better evaluate the playwright's worth by seeing what he did with a familiar tale. What he stressed, how he stressed it, how he restructured the familiar elements — these were the important matters. Shakespeare closely followed Sir Thomas North's very popular translation of Plutarch's *Life of Marcus Antonius*, for example, in writing *Antony and Cleopatra*; and he modified Robert Greene's *Pandosto* and combined it with the Pygmalion myth in *The Winter's Tale*, while drawing the character of Autolycus from certain pamphlets written by Greene. The only plays for which sources have not been clearly determined are *Love's Labour's Lost* (probably based on contemporary events) and *The Tempest* (possibly based on some shipwreck account from travellers to the New World).

Verse and Prose

There is a mixture of verse and prose in the plays, partially because plays fully in verse were out of fashion. Greater variety could thus be achieved and character or atmosphere could be more precisely delineated. Elevated passages, philosophically significant ideas, speeches by men of high rank are in verse, but comic and light parts, speeches including dialect or broken English, and scenes that move more rapidly or simply give mundane information are in prose. The poetry is almost always blank verse (iambic pentameter lines without rhyme). Rhyme is used, however (particularly the couplet), to mark the close of scenes or an important action. Rhyme also serves as a cue for the entrance of another actor or some off-stage business, to point to a change of mood or thought, as a forceful opening after a passage of prose, to convey excitement or passion or sentimentality and to distinguish characters.

Shakespeare's plays may be divided into three general categories, though some plays are not readily classified and further subdivisions may be suggested within a category.

The History Play

The history play, or chronicle, may tend to tragedy, like *Richard II*, or to comedy, like *Henry IV*, Part I. It is a chronicle of some royal personage, often altered for dramatic purposes, even to the point of falsification of the facts. Its popularity may have resulted from the rising of nationalism of the English, nurtured by their successes against the Spanish, their developing trade and colonization, and their rising prestige as a world power. The chronicle was considered a political guide, like the popular *Mirror for Magistrates*, a collection of writings showing what happens when an important leader falls through some error in his ways, his thinking or his personality. Thus the history play counseled the right path by negative, if not positive, means. Accordingly, it is difficult to call *Richard II* a tragedy, since Richard was wrong and his wrongness harmed his people. The political philosophy of Shakespeare's day seemed to favor the view that all usurpation was bad and should be corrected, but not by further usurpation. When that original usurpation had been established, through an heir's ascension to the throne, it was to be accepted. Then any rebellion against the "true" king would be a rebellion against God.

Tragedy

Tragedy in simple terms meant that the protagonist died. Certain concepts drawn from Aristotle's *Poetics* require a tragic hero of high standing, who must oppose some conflicting force, either external or internal. The tragic hero should be dominated by a *hamartia* (a so-called tragic flaw, but really an *excess* of some character trait, e.g., pride, or *hubris*), and it is this *hamartia* that leads to his downfall and, because of his status, to the downfall of others. The action presented in the tragedy must be recognizable to the audience as real and potential: through seeing it enacted, the audience has its passion (primarily suffering) raised, and the conclusion of the action thus brings release from that passion (*catharsis*). A more meaningful way of looking at tragedy in the Elizabethan theater, however, is to see it as that which occurs when essential good (like Hamlet) is wasted (through disaster or death) in the process of driving out evil (such as Claudius represents).

Comedy

Comedy in simple terms meant that the play ended happily for the protagonists. Sometimes the comedy depends on exaggerations of man's eccentricities — comedy of humors; sometimes the comedy is romantic and far-fetched. The romantic comedy was usually based on a mix-up in events or confused identity of characters, particularly by disguise. It moved toward tragedy in that an important person might die and the mix-up might never be unraveled; but in the nick of time something happens or someone appears (sometimes illogically or unexpectedly) and saves the day. It reflects the structure of myth by moving from happiness to despair to resurrection. *The Winter's Tale* is a perfect example of this, for the happiness of the first part is banished with Hermione's exile and Perdita's abandonment; tragedy is near when the lost baby, Perdita, cannot be found and Hermione is presumed dead, but Perdita reappears, as does Hermione, a statue that suddenly comes to life. Lost identities are established and confusions disappear but the mythic-comic nature of the play is seen in the reuniting of the mother, Hermione, a kind of Ceres, with her daughter, Perdita, a kind of Prosperina. Spring returns, summer will bring the harvest, and the winter of the tale is left behind — for a little while.

What is it, then, that makes Shakespeare's art so great? Perhaps we see in it a whole spectrum of humanity, treated impersonally, but with kindness and understanding. We seldom meet in Shakespeare a weeping philosopher: he may criticize, but he criticizes both sides. After he has done so, he gives the impression of saying, Well, that's the way life is; people will always be like that — don't get upset about it. This is probably the key to the Duke's behavior in *Measure for Measure* — a most unbitter comedy despite former labels. Only in *Hamlet* does Shakespeare not seem to fit this statement; it is the one play that Shakespeare, the person, enters.

As we grow older and our range of experience widens, so, too, does Shakespeare's range seem to expand. Perhaps this lies in the ambiguities of his own materials, which allow for numerous individual readings. We meet our own experiences — and they are ours alone, we think — expressed in phrases that we thought our own or of our own discovery. What makes Shakespeare's art so great, then, is his ability to say so much to so many people in such memorable language: he is himself "the show and gaze o' the time."

ANTONY and CLEOPATRA
Plot Summary

After the murder of Julius Caesar, the Roman Empire was ruled by three men, the noble triumvirs, Mark Antony, Lepidus, and Octavius Caesar, Julius Caesar's nephew. Antony, having been given the Eastern sphere to rule, had gone to Alexandria and there he had seen and fallen passionately in love with Cleopatra, Queen of Egypt. She was the flower of the Nile, but a wanton woman who had been the mistress of Julius Caesar and of many others. Antony was so filled with lust for her that he ignored his own counsel and the warnings of his friends, and as long as possible he also ignored a request from Octavius Caesar that he return to Rome. Sextus Pompeius, son of Pompey the Great, and a powerful leader, was gathering troops to seize Rome from the rule of the triumvirs, and Octavius Caesar wished to confer with the other two, Antony and Lepidus. At last the danger of a victory by Sextus Pompeius, coupled with the news that his wife Fulvia was dead, forced Antony to leave Egypt and Cleopatra and journey to Rome.

Pompeius was confident of victory so long as Antony stayed in Egypt, for Antony was a better general than either Lepidus or Caesar. When Pompeius heard that Antony was headed toward Rome, his hope was that Caesar and Antony would not mend their quarrels but would continue to fight each other as they had in the past. Lepidus did not matter; he sided with neither of the other two, and cared little for conquest and glory. Pompeius faced disappointment, however, for Antony and Caesar mended their quarrels in the face of common danger. To seal their renewed friendship, Antony married Octavia, the sister of Octavius Caesar; through her, each general would be bound to the other. Thus it seemed that Pompeius' scheme to separate Antony and Caesar would fail. His last hope was that Antony's lust would send him back to Cleopatra; then he and Caesar would battle each other and Pompeius would conquer Rome. To stall for time, he sealed a treaty with the triumvirs. Antony, with his wife, went to Athens on business for the Empire. There, word reached him that Pompeius and Caesar had waged war in spite of the treaty they had signed, and Pompeius had been killed. Caesar's next move was to seize Lepidus on the pretext that he had aided Pompeius. Now the Roman world had but two rulers, Caesar and Antony.

But Antony could not resist the lure of Cleopatra. Sending Octavia, his wife, home from Athens, he hurried back to Egypt. His return ended all pretence of friendship between him and Caesar. Each man prepared for battle, the winner to be the sole ruler of the world. Cleopatra joined her forces with those of Antony. At first Antony was supreme on the land, but Caesar ruled the sea and lured Antony to fight him there. Antony's friends and captains, particularly loyal Enobarbus, begged him not to risk his forces on the sea, but Antony, confident of victory,

15

prepared to match his ships with those of Caesar at Actium. In the decisive hour of the great sea fight Cleopatra ordered her fleet to leave the battle and sail for home. Antony, leaving the battle and his honor and his glory, followed her. Because he had set the example for desertion, many of his men left his forces and joined the standard of Caesar.

Antony was sunk in gloom at the folly of his own actions, but his lust had made him drunk with desire, and everything, even honor, must bow to Cleopatra. She protested that she did not know that Antony would follow her when she sailed away. Antony had reason enough to know she lied, but he still wanted her at any cost.

Caesar sent word to Cleopatra that she might have all her wishes granted if she would surrender Antony to Caesar. Knowing that Caesar was likely to be the victor in the struggle, she sent him a message of loyalty and of admiration for his greatness. Although Antony had seen her receive the addresses of Caesar's messenger, and even though he ranted and stormed at her for her faithlessness, she was easily able to dispel his fears and jealousy and make him hers again. After a failure to sue for peace, Antony decided to march again against his enemy. At this decision even the faithful Enobarbus left him and went over to Caesar, for he thought Antony had lost his reason as well as his honor. But Enobarbus too was an honorable man who shortly afterward died of shame for deserting his general.

On the day of the battle, victory was in sight for Antony, in spite of overwhelming odds. But once more the flight of the Egyptian fleet betrayed him. His defeat left Caesar master of the world. Antony was like a madman, seeking nothing but revenge on treacherous Cleopatra. When the queen heard of his rage, she had word sent to him that she was dead, killed by her own hand out of love for him. Convinced once more that Cleopatra had been true to him, Antony called on Eros, his one remaining follower, to kill him so that he could join Cleopatra in death. But faithful Eros killed himself rather than stab his beloved general. Determined to die, Antony fell on his own sword. Even that desperate act was without dignity or honor, for he did not die immediately and he could find no one who loved him enough to end his pain and misery. While he lay there, a messenger brought word that Cleopatra still lived. He ordered his servants to carry him to her. There he died in her arms, each proclaiming love for the other.

When Octavius Caesar heard the news of Antony's death, he grieved. Although he had fought and conquered Antony, he lamented the sorry fate of a great man turned weakling, ruined by his own lust. He sent a messenger to assure Cleopatra that she would be treated royally, that she should be ruler of her own fate. But the queen learned, as Antony had warned her, that Caesar would take her to Rome to march behind him in his triumphant procession, where she, a queen and mistress to two former rulers of the world, would be pinched and spat upon by rabble and slaves. To cheat him of his triumph, she put on her crown and all her royal garb, placed a poisonous asp on her breast, and lay down to die. Charmian and Iras, her loyal attendants, died the same death. Octavius Caesar, entering her chamber, saw her dead, but as beautiful and desirable as in life. There was only one thing he could do for his one-time friend and the dead queen: he ordered their burial in a common grave, together in death as they had wished to be in life.

Sources of the Play

The sources to which Shakespeare turned for the plots of his dramas were extremely varied. English chronicle-history, Italian novels, Roman history — all are skilfully used with results that reflect the highest achievement of dramatic genius.

Those plays whose subjects are drawn from the history of Rome are conveniently called the Roman plays. They are *Julius Caesar*, *Antony and Cleopatra*, *Coriolanus*, and *Timon of Athens*. In all four cases, Shakespeare's direct source was a famous work of Sir Thomas North entitled *Plutarch's Lives of the Noble Grecians and Romans*, though the debt in the case of *Timon of Athens* was much smaller than that of the other three plays mentioned. North's book, published in 1579, was a translation of a French work by James Amyot, who himself translated from the original work of Plutarch, a Greek writer of the first century after Christ.

The extent to which Shakespeare, in *Antony and Cleopatra*, is indebted to North's work is very considerable, though not so great as in the case of *Julius Caesar*. In some cases, a hint given by Plutarch in the *Life of Antonius* is incorporated in the play; in many other cases, whole pages of North's translation are embodied in the dramatic version, the very word order being sometimes reproduced. But, in nearly every case, the appropriation of incidents from North has been accomplished with such dramatic skill, and they have been presented with such poetic imagery and fancy, that the product is Shakespeare's and his alone. Moreover, Shakespeare's art is shown, not only in the handling of the material chosen, but in the previous selection of it. Apart from one or two isolated cases where his adherence to his original has led to the introduction of superfluous and undramatic details, the selection of incidents throwing light upon the characters of the principal persons in the drama, in their individual lives as well as in their relations among themselves, shows admirable judgment. The following scheme presents the main points in which Shakespeare has adopted the facts of North's book.

1. Events of Main Historical Importance

(a) The meeting between Antony and Cleopatra at the River Cydnus (Act II, Sc. 2).

(b) The treaty of Misenum, and the plot of Menas (Act II, Sc. 6 & 7).

(c) The fight at Actium, and flight of Cleopatra, followed by Antony (Act III, Sc. 6, Sc. 7, Sc. 10, Sc. 11).

(d) Antony's death; Cleopatra's retreat to her monument, and death (Act IV, Sc. 13, Sc. 14, Sc. 15; Act I, Sc. 2).

2. Events of Less Historical Importance

(a) The war of Lucius and Fulvia against Caesar (Act I, Sc. 2).

(b) Sextus' command of the sea (Act I, Sc. 4).

(c) The arrangement ending in the marriage of Antony and Octavia (Act II, Sc. 2).

(d) Ventidius and the Parthians (Act II, Sc. 3; Act III, Sc. 1).

(e) Desertion of Domitius (Act IV, Sc. 4 and 9).

(f) The battles in Egypt (Act IV, Sc. 10 and 12).

(g) Caesar's interview with Cleopatra (Act V, Sc. 2).

3. Incidents Bearing Upon Personal Character

(a) Antony's descent (Act I, Sc. 3), popularity with soldiers (Act I, Sc. 4) and servants (Act IV, Sc. 2), endurance (Act I, Sc. 4), superstitious nature (Act II, Sc. 3), jealousy of Cleopatra (Act II, Sc. 5, Act III, Sc. 12 and 13) and of Caesar (Act III, Sc. 4 *et passim*), fatuous devotion to Cleopatra (Act I, Sc. 1 and 4), thought for friends (Act III, Sc. 11).

(b) Cleopatra's voluptuous nature (Act II, Sc. 2; Act III, Sc. 6 and 13) and vanity (Act I, Sc. 5; Act III, Sc. 6), her passion for love and hate, her allurements (*passim*), her cowardice (Act III, Sc. 10 and 11), her display of spirit at the end (Act II, Sc. 5).

(c) Octavia's goodness, her patience, her miserable lot (Act III, Sc. 4).

(d) Caesar's sternness, inflexibility of purpose, impatience of rivalry, coldness and absence of passion.

The greatest dependence on North is shown in the Fourth and Fifth Acts, where most of the incidents originate with his work. Important exceptions are the last half of Act IV, Sc. 15, the vision of Act V, Sc. 2, 76-100 and the wonderful piece of dramatic writing in Act V, Sc. 2.

Date of Production

The play, first registered in 1608 and printed in the Folio of 1623, seven years after Shakespeare's death, belongs to the last period of his production. Internal evidences of its being a late play are as follows: 1, the absence of rhyme, used everywhere in early plays and gradually disappearing as new ones were produced; 2, the presence of numerous weak or light endings of lines which increased in number in the last plays; 3, condensation of thought and absence of long passages of description or philosophy; and 4, moderation in treatment of tragic themes — there is an absence of gruesome details such as we find in Macbeth and Julius Caesar. Here battles are spoken of, not exhibited; there is no agony of death displayed, except perhaps in the case of Antony's failure in killing himself directly; the deaths of Enobarbus, Cleopatra, and her women are more graceful than horrible.

The World of *Antony and Cleopatra*

The world we live in, that is, the environmental surroundings, are neutral facts of existence. They, in and by themselves, have no particular point-of-view. But when we, as men, come to this world we inevitably feel the compulsion to form it into something that reflects our personalities. This conception which we force the neutral, physical world to assume is one of several ways of defining the world of the play. It is the philosophical world or the psychological world depending upon which element is emphasized by the writer. In Shakespeare there is a very complete and harmonious blending of the philosophical with the psychological. If we take the three worlds of the play in order of importance from least to most significant, it would probably be as follows: the physical world (the physical environment of Egypt and Rome and their differences); the psychological world (the world that deals with the relationship of the person to the world of the senses); and the philosophical world (the universe of ideas). It is valuable for the student of the play to keep in mind these three ways of looking at the finished work. For the purpose of discussion it is important to be able to speak about them separately, even though Shakespeare certainly never did so. In his mind there probably was no such division of the elements; his mind thought on all these levels at the same time.

The Physical World

The action of the play takes place from the death of Fulvia to the death of Cleopatra. There are two very different physical worlds contrasted within the limits of the first and last scenes. The first of these worlds, and the most important, is Egypt. It is here that Antony's heart really belongs and longs to remain. Cleopatra's palace is at Alexandria, on the delta of the Nile River. The scene is thus set under a hot and burning sun, in a strange country (strange to Rome and to Elizabethan England), amidst many strange creatures and ideas. Within the imagery of the play we hear of the crocodile, the asp, the dolphin, the flooding of the Nile, figs, the goddess Isis, eunuchs, luxurious nights of revelry, palm trees, tears and sighs, etc. The historical time of the play's action is the year 30 B.C. There are also scenes at Rome in Acts I, II and III. Rome was the ruling center of the ancient world.

Upon the death of Marcus Brutus, a triumvirate was formed to divide and rule this world. Eventually it included Octavius Caesar, Marcus Antonius, and Lepidus, all three generals of the army. The unity of the ancient world was dependent upon the harmonious working together of these three generals. Frequently, though, this harmony broke down from within or was challenged from without, as in this case by Sextus Pompeius. Then wars occurred and the victors divided up the spoils and tried to rule again. This time the war resulted in the dictatorship of Octavius Caesar, who took the name of Augustus upon his succession. The minor scenes take place at Athens and in Syria. Thus the play encompasses the entire Mediterranean area. This is the physical world of *Antony and Cleopatra*, the entire ancient world.

The World Shaped by the Characters

The physical world greatly determines the world shaped by the numerous Egyptian and Roman characters. There is a major conflict between the world of sensuousness and luxury, a world made for love and languishing (Egypt) and a world of duty and soldiership, of stoicism, and of politics and power (Rome). Cleopatra is the symbol of the former and Caesar the symbol of the latter. Antony is caught between them and suffers the pangs of conscience and guilt of someone caught in such a conflict. He had been one of the greatest generals in the ancient world and shared in the division of its power. He had also come under the spell of Egypt and had succumbed to its influence. But the conflict goes deeper. As Shakespeare sees it, Egypt represents a world of imagination and words. Thus it is a world of the mind and of romantic feelings. Rome is a world of practical affairs and power politics. Caesar cannot afford the luxury of too keen a sense of feeling for beauty and refinement. At best he loves his sister, Octavia, but he is willing to sacrifice her to political expediency by marrying her to Antony. He has little good to say for his opponent Antony until after his death. Then, when he is out of the way, he can afford a few words of appreciation. His world is also the world of youth, the only world that has the strength and energy to become involved so completely in the fight for power. Antony, in the past, had also lived as a member of this Roman world, but he has now grown older and no longer has the youthful drive required to be a total success in it. His mind and way of thinking have changed and no longer function in the way Caesar's does. In maturity the mind and imagination turn to other realms. One of the conflicts for Antony until the end of the play is that he does not accept this fact of life. He still believes that his responsibility calls for him to support Caesar and Lepidus against Pompey, and in the sense that he is a member of the Triumvirate, it really does. The psychological world of the play is defined by this conflict of interest. His honor and reputation are still of prime importance to Antony. He does not become caught in the conflict until this honor is threatened by his relationship with Cleopatra. His jealousy and fierceness with words against his love are a product of this conflict of interest. She is the cause of his loss of reputation. She has kept him away from his rightful duties. Yet he loves her passionately and is unable to give her up permanently. The flaws in his character, his love of luxury, his softness of purpose, his quickness to blame others, are all a product of the impossibility of reconciling these conflicting points of view.

One of the glories of Shakespeare is that he never directly points to the psychology of a character. He always makes it a central part of the action, the all important events on which the framework of the play is hung. The audience, then, must emotionally respond to the inner lives of the characters in their own ways; they must feel the characters as if they were real, alive persons with their own unconscious motivations for acting as they do. Ultimately, whatever seemingly unresolvable problems a Shakespearean play presents must be settled within the mind of the audience on a non-verbal level. Thus, the vast number of different interpretations that any of his plays can support. The value of criticism is in the becoming aware of what other people, with the facility to verbalize their thoughts and emotional reactions, have experienced when confronted with the play. This experience, too, is predicated upon the era of history that the critic is living in. One era will stress the romantic elements, another the psychological elements, and a third the dramatic or even the ethical elements.

Reflecting the Real World

The real world, that is, the world beyond the realms of thought and feeling of any one person, is a composite of all the different points of view possible toward life. It is also something more that can only be experienced by living it. Shakespeare obviously had the capacity to live in this larger, transcendental world and to indicate his varying experience of it through his poetry. One essential of the real world is practical affairs. This aspect of it is present in the figure of Octavius Caesar, but it is ironically criticized by his emptiness of emotion. Pompey, while somewhat more ethical and decent than Caesar, is, consequently, less powerful and effective in achieving his aims. He doesn't "play the game" in the only way it can be won — ruthlessly. If this seems like a very modern opinion of politics, let it be understood that politics has changed very little since the time of Shakespeare, or even since the time of ancient Rome.

The contemporaneity of Shakespeare derives from his supreme ability to abstract the general and the lasting from the particular and momentary. Society has always had to deal with the conflict between imagination and practicality. And it has never been able to resolve the conflict satisfactorily. Few people have been able to rise to the heights of imagination that Antony and Cleopatra ascend to, but few people are also as basically honorable as he is. Antony is what Cleopatra calls him — a "heavenly mingle." The real tragedy is that even so magnificent a person as he is falls in the conflict with duty and responsibility. What Shakespeare further shows in the relationship between Cleopatra and her hero is the extreme anti-socialness of a consuming passion. For them no one or nothing else exists except each other. Until Antony feels the conflict, the world could go "hang." Since not all readers will appreciate and accept the Egyptian side of Antony's nature, it is fair to say that Shakespeare is saying that the realm of the imagination and poetry is as real as the purely practical, political world. It is certainly different, with its own rules and limitations, but it is as real. The problem is that it cannot exist in this world; it is pushed aside into death by the more immediate requirements of existence. When it becomes exclusive of the pressures of practical reality it leads to death. The physical world of Rome and Egypt may be very remote from today's audience, but the imagination of the characters is fully understandable in an emotional sense, even if the miracle of the writing is unfathomable.

Summaries and Commentaries by Act and Scene
ACT I · SCENE 1

Summary

The first scene of the play is set in the Palace of Cleopatra at Alexandria. Two friends of Mark Antony, Demetrius and Philo, are concerned with Antony's forsaking the ways of war for the pleasures of love. They feel that instead of commanding, he is commanded. As Antony and Cleopatra enter on their way to another night of revels, a Messenger appears with news from Rome. Antony, though, has so far forgotten his responsibilities as a military leader that he refuses to hear the Messenger. In slighting the Messenger he is showing disrespect to Octavius Caesar from whom he came. Antony and Cleopatra continue their verbal exchange on the theme of love and faithfulness, completely absorbed in themselves. After they leave, Antony's two friends comment on the scene which has just occurred, saying that Rumor was right, Antony is no longer himself.

Commentary

Nowhere is Shakespeare's mastery of the technique of the theatre more apparent than in his handling of opening scenes, and this is one of his most brilliant examples, compressing into a brief 62 lines the outlines of themes and characters that he will develop and elaborate throughout the rest of the play. Philo and Demetrius are Roman soldiers and Philo gives, as we might expect, the Roman view of Antony's situation: his love is "dotage." This would also be the view of those members of the audience who knew the story (a large number — the Elizabethan audience was not as illiterate as it is sometimes said to have been). At this point the audience could confidently expect a straightforward dramatization of a favorite Elizabethan theme, the moral failing and consequent downfall of a great man. But Shakespeare will offer them as well as the conventional interpretation, an alternate and opposing one. This will embody, if not a justification of the two lovers, at least a powerful suggestion that their passion has its own kind of virtue, not comprehended by the practical morality of Rome. The opening speech is also interesting from the point of view of dramatic technique. The Elizabethan theatre was a noisy and unruly place, and plays needed to open in a way that would catch the attention of the audience and subdue them. Shakespeare's device, here and in other plays, is to open in the middle of an excited conversational exchange. Philo's first words ("Nay, but...") are obviously in reply to something said by Demetrius. The audience is immediately alert: what is being said, and about whom?

Coming in the middle of Philo's denunciation, the entrance of the two principals at line 10 is an intensely dramatic one. Here (and throughout the play) the reader must imagine for himself the various possibilities of costume, grouping, movement, and staging generally. Here the stage direction is explicit: Antony and Cleopatra are preceded by a "flourish" (notes played on a trumpet), and surrounded by a crowd of supporters. While the Elizabethan stage was relatively bare, costumes could be lavish, and Antony and Cleopatra and their train would undoubtedly appear in rich and elaborate attire. This richness should be preserved in any staging, since it provides a significant visual contrast between the two principals and the two Roman soldiers, dressed in harsh Roman simplicity, who stand at the side of the stage, observing. The dramatic opposition between Egyptian voluptuousness and Roman hardness is made with neat economy through visual means. The Roman-Egypt contrast is made again, in a different form, at the entrance of the Messenger at line 17, bringing "news, my lord, from Rome." Throughout the first half of the play the action oscillates between Rome and Egypt, but we may note that in the Rome-scenes Egypt is represented in some way (e.g. Enobarbus' description of Cleopatra, Act II, Sc. 2) and in the Egypt-scenes Rome is also present (here, in the arrival of the Messenger). In Egypt we are made conscious of Rome, and in Rome, of Egypt. This reflects the conflict within Antony and, indeed, the conflict of the whole play.

There are two other important elements in this scene. The first is the introduction of Cleopatra. She must be made impressive, and Shakespeare achieves this by having her dominate Antony in their opening exchange. She will "set a bourn how far to be beloved," she chides Antony for dismissing the Messenger, and reminds him of his responsibilities to his wife, Fulvia, and "scarce-bearded" Caesar. The second point is Antony's own comment on the nature of his love for Cleopatra which is, in a sense, a reply to Philo's remarks about his "dotage." There is tremendous energy and confidence in his sweeping rejection of Rome (33-4), and all of worldly ambition — "Kingdoms are clay; our dungy earth alike/ Feeds beast as man." This confident affirmation will be shaken later ("I must from this enchanting queen break off," Act I, Sc. 2, 112), and just as the play moves back and forth between Rome and Egypt, so Antony's emotions are, at one point, those of Cleopatra's lover and, at the next, those of the endangered Roman general.

One of the central themes of the play is the inadequacy of the normal as a yardstick for measuring a relationship which is larger than life. The first exchange between Cleopatra and Antony expresses the inability of language to deal with the rare and exceptional experience:

23

Cleo: If it be love indeed, tell me how much.

Ant: There's beggary in the love that can be reckoned.

Cleo: I'll set a bourn how far to be beloved.

Ant: Then must thou needs find out new heaven,
new earth.   (lines 14-17)

The love between Antony and the Queen of the Nile is larger than the confines of this small earth. It is a world unto itself; it cannot be measured in words. The student will be aware how often the two lovers try to define the nature and extent of their love. He may begin to feel that what they say to each other is only the fanciful exaggeration of romance. But to think this would be to fail to experience the deepest level of the play wherein the world itself is too small a place to contain the magnificence that man can rise to. The Elizabethan drama was given to excesses of language and poetic imagery. The greatness of Shakespeare rests, partly, with the genius he had in finding the right images to convey the subtlest of human thoughts and feelings. He was rarely excessive in his use of words; behind every large image and metaphor is an experience of the world that is being pointed to through the language.

Both Cleopatra and Antony are aware of the uniqueness of their love and its incompatibility with a world which makes too many immediate and varied practical demands. When Antony says to Cleopatra:

No messenger but thine, and all alone
Tonight we'll wander through the streets and note
The qualities of people.   (lines 52-54)

he is admitting to their isolation from the world.

ACT I · SCENE 2

Summary

In this scene we meet first the female attendants of Cleopatra, who share to a lesser extent than she does the devotion to love. Second, we meet Enobarbus, Antony's closest friend. Charmian enquires of a Sooth-sayer her fate in life. She asks for a good fortune, and he replies (ambiguously as it turns out) that she will live longer than her mistress. The dialogue is filled with a delightful bawdiness and a hidden irony about the events to come. When Iras, another handmaiden, requests her fortune as well, she is told that it is to be the same as that of Charmian. Cleopatra interrupts the banter between Iras and Charmian. She has come in search of Antony, who had suddenly thought of the Messenger who had appeared in Scene 1, and left the banquet to find him. He and Antony appear as soon as the stage is empty. From the Messenger we learn that Fulvia, Antony's wife, has made war against Lucius; then, with peace re-established, they both turned against Octavius Caesar. The Parthians have also attacked the Empire, successfully conquering the eastern reaches of Rome. Antony is made aware of the decline in his reputation

24

as a result of his lingering in Egypt with Cleopatra. Another Messenger brings the news that Fulvia is dead. Antony expresses feelings of both satisfaction at her removal and sorrow that "a great spirit (is) gone!" He makes a resolution to leave Egypt and return to his rightful place as one of the Triumvirate. He applies to himself the same criticism of falling into dotage that the two soldiers made in the opening of Scene 1. When Enobarbus returns and learns that Antony means to leave Egypt, he warns him that this will kill Cleopatra. She is made only for love and cannot bear the loss of it. Antony tells him of Fulvia's death and of the trouble she has stirred up. Enobarbus speaks lightly of her death and is reproved by Antony. Sextus Pompeius, the youngest son of Pompey the Great, has challenged Octavius Caesar, and actually has control of the seas. Antony says he must leave Egypt.

Commentary

The first thing we notice in this scene is that the dialogue has moved from verse to prose. In part, this is done to give the audience a change from the rhythm of five-beat iambic pentameter, which can become monotonous when sustained over long periods. But it also indicates a change of mood. These are subordinate characters, jesting in a relaxed uninhibited fashion: in Shakespeare such conversations are usually given the free, informal structure of prose.

It is also significant that the scene's first 82 lines add nothing to the development of the plot. Such sequences are frequent in Shakespeare's plays, and they do not mean that he was a sloppy or uneconomical playwright. They are there, not to advance the story, but to develop a theme or imaginative setting. We have heard, from Philo, of Cleopatra's "gypsy's lust." This conversation among the members of her retinue elaborates this notion of Egyptian voluptuousness, or the "Egyptian motif" of the play and, on the bare stage of the Elizabethan theater, constructs a verbal setting for Cleopatra. Wine is brought in, "enough Cleopatra's health to drink," and a good deal of the dialogue that follows revolves around adultery and sexual promiscuity. The emphasis is on sensuality, on sexual activity which is totally divorced from morality. Value, in Egypt, is equated with the satisfaction of appetite. Although it is Charmian and Iras who talk, this is, by implication, the value that Cleopatra represents.

There are two other points of interest in the first phase of the scene. The first concerns the Soothsayer. Shakespeare often introduces such characters: they are said to have prophetic powers, and they say things which carry an ominous meaning, understood by the audience, but not by the characters in the play. This device reminds us of the characters' ultimate fate (since we know the story), and underlines their ignorance of it. When, for example, the Soothsayer tells Charmian and Iras that their "former fortune" is "fairer" than "that which is to approach" (32), and that their "fortunes are alike," we realize that his words apply to their deaths, together, in Act V, Sc. 2. They do not know this, but for a moment the frivolity of the scene is overshadowed by the approaching tragedy.

The second point concerns Enobarbus. He occupies an important role in the play, and Shakespeare is always careful about the introduction of important characters. Enobarbus says very little here, but what he does say is significant. First he calls for wine (11) and then, as the ladies ask for their fortunes to be told, he sourly remarks that "most of our fortunes, to-night, shall be — drunk to bed" (43). In these remarks the foundation of his character is laid, and it will be developed later. He is a soldier, ready to take whatever pleasures come his way: he can drink, and enjoy, the Egyptian wine with none of the moral disapproval of such Romans as Philo and Demetrius. He is also a realist, and perhaps something of a cynic. Beneath the gaiety, the word-play, the indecent innuendo of the Alexandrian court he sees the basic self-indulgence — "drunk to bed" — and is, at least for the time being, happy to put up with it. We shall see later how this cynical, hard-headed realism is tested by the approach of Antony's destruction.

At 74 Cleopatra enters for a brief 10 lines, allowing for some sharpening of the focus on her character. Note first that her interest is concentrated totally on Antony, although she has, in our first view of her, behaved with coolness toward him. Secondly, she is well aware of the contradiction between his affection in Egypt and his obligation in Rome; the phrase "a Roman thought hath struck him" is spoken with real fear of his possible abandonment of her. Yet when he does arrive, and although she has sent for him, she "will not look upon him," and quits the stage. She is a consummate actress, and takes every opportunity to baffle, frustrate, and confuse her lover: tactics which will, in the end, bring about his death. Yet it is difficult to disapprove of Cleopatra as it is to condemn morally any great natural force. We begin to see why the critics have called her "a courtesan of genius."

In much of the remainder of this scene (the exception being Antony's exchange with Enobarbus over Fulvia's death) Shakespeare fills in the necessary plot development. We may compare his dramatic foreshortening with his source, Plutarch: "Now Antonius delighting in these fond and childish pastimes, very ill news was brought him from two places. The first from Rome, that his brother Lucius and Fulvia his wife fell out first between themselves, and afterwards fell to open war with Caesar, and had brought all to nought, that they were both driven to fly out of Italy. The second news, as bad as the first: that Labienus conquered all Asia with the army of the Parthians, from the river of Euphrates and from Syria unto the countries of Lydia and Ionia. Then began Antonius with much ado a little to rouse himself, as if he had been wakened out of a deep sleep, and, as a man say, coming out of a great drunkenness . . ."

Our view of Antony is somewhat enlarged in this scene. Until now we have only seen him with Cleopatra, and enthralled by her. Here we get a glimpse of Antony the "triple pillar" of the world, a man of stature and decision. He asks that the messenger give him an honest account of how things stand at Rome (92), and is suddenly aware, with cold clarity, of the insecurity of his position in the Triumvirate. This is accompanied by a realization of the danger of his obsession with Cleopatra: "These strong Egyptian fetters I must break/ or lose myself in dotage." It is significant that Antony himself uses the world Philo applied to him in the play's first line. We recall that he is, himself, a Roman, and from time to time in the play sees himself through Roman eyes.

ACT I · SCENE 3

Summary

The last scene having ended with Antony's preparation to leave, this scene opens with Cleopatra's search for him. She sends Charmian to find him and with a message to tell him that she is happy if Charmian finds him sad, and sad if she finds him happy. Before she can leave, Antony arrives to say his farewell. She is in a mood of playful rebellion against Antony, not having forgotten the first news about Fulvia, but not yet knowing that she has died. She pretends that he has betrayed her and does not immediately see Antony's disinclination to be jocular. He tries to explain to her, but she keeps interrupting him with her mock accusations. When he finally has a chance to tell her that he must be off to Rome and that Fulvia has died, Cleopatra's mood suddenly deepens and she finds it difficult to say what is really in her heart.

Commentary

Cleopatra's opening question reminds us that, however she may behave in Antony's presence, her actions and emotions are totally concentrated on him. We are also given, in 2-5, a compressed exemplification of what we may call her amorous tactics with regard to him. To paraphrase: "I must know everything about him, where he is, who he wants to be with, the kind of thing he wants to do. But he must not know of my concern. Whatever his mood, disrupt it by telling him that I feel just the opposite, since I must maintain control over his emotions." Charmian's objection would occur to all of us: can this kind of emotional manipulation really be love? But Cleopatra immediately rejects her urging to be suppliant and obedient — "Thou teachest like a fool: the way to lose him!" (10). We may compare this attitude to that of Shakespeare's younger heroines in love, for example Juliet, whose innocence would make her quite incapable of such calculated manoeuvering. But Cleopatra is neither young nor innocent. In the dialogue which follows with Antony she commands the stage, guessing at Antony's intention of announcing his departure. She threatens to faint (the last thing we would imagine her doing here), rails at the control "the married woman" has over Antony, and denounces the falsity of his "mouth-made vows."

Antony, in this part of the dialogue, is limited to hopeless attempts at interrupting this flow of invective: "my dearest queen— . . . The gods best know— . . . Cleopatra— . . . Most sweet queen— . . ." Not until 41 does he succeed in making himself heard.

The speech in which Antony describes the situation which obliges him to return to Rome has been discussed by D.A. Traversi (*An Approach to Shakespeare*) in a passage which is both illuminating in itself, and provides a good example of the close critical analysis of Shakespeare's text. "It would be hard to find a better example of the way in which what can easily be read as no more than a straightforward piece of exposition is in fact charged with a linguistic vitality that relates it variously to the deeper issues of the play. Rome is in a dangerous state of 'equality,' poised between two powers which, uncertain of the future and unable to trust one another, 'breed' (the verb, with its sense of organic growth, has a quality of its own) a 'scrupulous,' calculating 'faction.' Pompey, in turn, the common enemy of Caesar and Antony, is 'rich' only in his father's reputation: thus speciously endowed, he 'creeps' by a process of stealthy treachery into the hearts of those who have not made their fortunes, 'thrives' in the 'present' state of deceptive peace. These, as a result, grow (through the 'breeding' process already defined, we might say) into a threatening condition, and the result of the whole development is summed up in one of those images of dislocated organic function by which Shakespeare, from *Henry IV* at least onwards, has habitually chosen to express the implications of civil strife. The discontented elements in Rome are 'sick': 'sick' in themselves, because domestic war was the symptom of political disorder, and 'sick' too of the false state of 'rest,' or stagnation, by which other interests in turn prosper. The end of this sickness here, as ever, is a 'purge,' but one scarcely less uncertain, 'desperate' in its possible consequences, than that the desire for which had inspired Northumberland and his fellow conspirators to action in the Second Part of *Henry IV*."

The rest of the scene is given over to the announcement of Fulvia's death to Cleopatra, and to the leave-taking. Cleopatra, in a characteristic and daring piece of argument, is able to turn Antony's loss to her own advantage: his lack of feeling for Fulvia's death shows her, she says, "how mine received shall be." It is a breathtaking example of egotism and impertinence, and throws more light on her remarkable character. She continues to chide Antony until, at his cold "I'll leave you, lady," she realizes she may have gone too far. Her final speech, though still concerned with her own loss ("be deaf to my unpitied folly"), is a reaffirmation of her love for Antony.

ACT I · SCENE 4

Summary

Having established the conflict which Antony is caught in, Shakespeare changes the scene to Rome. We first encounter Octavius Caesar reading a letter. Apparently, the letter is news from Alexandria, informing Caesar of the way that Antony is behaving there with Cleopatra. Caesar sums up the opinion held of Antony at Rome and expresses some displeasure at the way Antony received Caesar's Messenger. Lepidus, the third member of the Triumvirate, responds with a mild defense of Antony, but he is called too indulgent by Caesar. Antony's wantonness would be all right did the times not demand that he give it up and come to the aid of his fellow rulers. It is this, and not Antony's success in love, that disturbs Caesar. A Messenger appears with further news. Caesar now learns what Antony learned in Scene 2: Pompey has been successful at sea, and men who are disaffected with Caesar or have reason to seek revenge against Julius for what he did to Pompey the Great, have gone over to Sextus Pompeius and swell his ranks. Not only is there bad news concerning Pompey, but we learn that two pirates of great repute, Menecrates and Menas, have taken advantage of the situation to attack the coasts of Italy, putting the inhabitants into a fear. Caesar, in despair at this news, begs out loud to the absent Antony that he should leave his luxury behind and take up the soldier's role that fits him best. He recalls some past exploits of Antony where in the worst circumstances he proved himself the best of soldiers. Lepidus says that he will let Caesar know on the next day just what he will be able to supply in the way of men and ships to the coming war with Pompey. As he is about to leave on this mission, he reminds Caesar to let him know whatever further news he should hear from abroad. Caesar assures Lepidus that he knew well enough that it was his duty to do so, and the scene ends.

Commentary

The first three scenes have taken place in Alexandria, but were full of references to Rome; now the action of the play moves to Rome and, as we might expect, the concern there is with Antony in Alexandria. Caesar is introduced, and his opening speeches reveal at least two qualities of the man which will be in evidence elsewhere in the play. In the first place he is given a formal, precise, even priggish manner. He addresses Lepidus almost as though he were delivering a lecture ("You may see . . . and henceforth know") and his reference to himself at line 2 has a touch of self-righteousness. Secondly, what he has to say about Antony shows him to be a prime representative of Roman moral rectitude. His language has a powerful overtone of disgust — "keep the turn of tippling with a slave . . . reel the streets . . . knaves that smell of sweat." Antony's passion ("the nobleness of life" in Act I, Sc. 1) is degraded to "to tumble on the bed of Ptolemy." Shakespeare borrows again from Plutarch for the substance of what Caesar says: "For Cleopatra (were it in sport, or in matters of earnest) still devised sundry new delights to have Antonius at commandment, never leaving him night or day, nor once letting him go out of her sight. For she would play at dice with him, drink with him, and hunt commonly with him, and also be with him when he went to any exercise of activity of body....Now though most men disliked his manner, yet the Alexandrians were commonly glad of this jollity, and liked it well, saying very gallantly and wisely: 'that Antonius showed them a comical face, to wit, a merry countenance: and the Roman a tragical face, to say, a grim look.' But to reckon up all the foolish sports they made, revelling in this sort, it were too fond a part of me...." We may also note, in this extract, the way in which Shakespeare has enlarged on the idea of implicit conflict between the "merry countenance" of Alexandrian pleasure-seeking, and the "grim look" of Rome.

One of Shakespeare's problems, particularly in the first three acts of the play, is to keep us aware of Antony's greatness. With Antony in the toils of Cleopatra, this is not always easy to do. One method is to recall his former greatness, which Caesar does at lines 55-71. The play shows us, in the first three scenes, an Antony apparently besotted by the sensual delights of Alexandria. In direct contrast is this account of the rigorous and physical ruggedness of his earlier military campaigns. We are reminded that Antony has suffered "more than savages could suffer," and that whatever delicacies he may enjoy in Egypt now, he was once forced to drink "the gilded puddle" and eat "the roughest berry on the rudest hedge." We are dealing with someone who has, in his time, been much more than a self-indulgent sensualist and will, at the play's end, be much more again.

ACT I · SCENE 5

Summary

Shakespeare returns us to Alexandria for a glimpse of the effect Antony's absence has had on Cleopatra. With Antony away, the theme of discussion between Cleopatra and Charmian turns to love-making and the eunuch, Mardian, gets involved in the witty word play which disguises Cleopatra's desire and longing for her lover. Antony becomes the measure for everything that happens. She tries to imagine where he is at that moment and what he is doing and who are so lucky to be with him when she is not. Alexas, a servant of Cleopatra, returns from Antony with a gift and words of endearment for her, Antony's gift is a pearl which he has kissed many times before sending it. The servant reports that Antony was neither sad nor happy as he went off on his horse, and Cleopatra takes this as an example of Antony's perfection. Remembering her affair with Julius Caesar, she asks Charmian if she ever bestowed so much love on Caesar. She and Charmian then engage in a playful exchange on the virtues of Caesar versus those of Antony. Cleopatra admits that the days with Caesar were but days of youth when she "was green in judgment, cold in blood."

Commentary

This is the first of several scenes in which we find Cleopatra in

Egypt, waiting for news of Antony. They do little to forward the plot, but are dramatically important in the development of Cleopatra's problem, peculiar to the Elizabethan stage. We must keep in mind that Shakespeare created his Cleopatra with a boy actor in mind (as she herself reminds us at Act V, Sc. 2, 220): "And I shall see/ Some squeaking Cleopatra boy my greatness"). This raises certain obvious difficulties in the Antony-Cleopatra scenes. Situations that would, with male and female actors, lead naturally to physical contact and embracing are impossible, since the spectacle of Antony embracing an adolescent boy would completely destroy the theatrical illusion. This accounts for the play's lack of physical "love scenes" in the sense that we understand them in contemporary drama and film. Yet at the same time Shakespeare must communicate the intensity of Antony's and Cleopatra's passion, and also, most difficult of all, must show us a Cleopatra who is superlatively desirable. Today this could be done through the obvious visual attractions of an actress, but Shakespeare must rely on the medium of language. He may use other characters' descriptions (as in Enobarbus' speech at Act II, Sc. 2, 191), or Cleopatra's speeches when, as here, she is apart from Antony, and her longing must remain unsatisfied. As usual, her preoccupation with Antony when he is absent is made clear immediately. His absence is a "great gap of time," and Charmian's remark that this preoccupation is excessive is nothing less than "treason." The tenor of what she says is predominantly sexual. Her exchange with Mardian the eunuch, while it does nothing to recommend Cleopatra as an example of civility or good taste, does reinforce our sense of her as representing (in this mood at least) an instinctive and overpowering sexuality. Again, she is the opposite of such innocent and virginal heroines as Juliet. She seems to feel this herself, and revel in the knowledge. She is the "serpent of old Nile" with "amorous pinches black." She recapitulates her conquests of "broad-fronted Caesar" and "great Pompey," and we believe her when she says, with obvious satisfaction, that she has been "a morsel for a monarch." There is also an undercurrent of violence in Cleopatra's language. She will give Charmian "bloody teeth" for saying that Caesar was Antony's equal, and she will send a messenger to Antony every day even if it means that she must "unpeople" Egypt. This violence both prepares us for her treatment of the Messenger at Act II, Sc. 5, and suggests the willful, forceful nature of her personality.

ACT II · SCENE 1

Summary

It is not until the sixth scene of the play (the original play was not divided into acts) that we meet the man who is the cause of all the struggle that the play centers on. We are in Messina at Pompey's house. Pompey is conferring with two of his allies, the pirates Menas and Menecrates. The reason which Pompey gives for waging war against the Triumvirate is that of retributive justice. Octavius Caesar's uncle, and father by adoption, Julius Caesar, wrested control of the Empire from Pompey the Great, the present Pompey's father, and he means to win it back. Control of the seas lies with him and many of the people have already taken his side. He is aware of the division in the ruling power that Caesar has been anxious to heal, and he knows that this will work to his own benefit, provided that Antony remains languishing in Egypt. Even Pompey recognizes that Antony is the man to be wary of. As a soldier, there is no other like him in the entire world. A follower of Pompey, Varrius, arrives with the bad news, which Pompey had denied the moment before, that Antony has left Egypt and returned to Rome to join forces with Caesar and Lepidus. Pompey is visibly affected by this unwelcome news. Menas reminds Pompey that there is enmity between Caesar and Antony over the wars started by Antony's wife, Fulvia. Pompey, the more clear-sighted, knows that faced with an outside enemy to their power they will make up their differences and band together.

Commentary

This interlude with Pompey and his followers roughs out as much of the historical outline of events as the audience needs at this point. Pompey congratulates himself on the growth of his own power, but Menas's information that Caesar and Lepidus are "in the field," and the arrival of Varrius with the news that Antony has left Egypt for Rome damps his optimism. The audience need not, in fact, know the historical details. What is important, at this point in the play, is that it be made to feel the quickening into action of the struggle for power. In Act I the Rome-Egypt contrast was made clear, and we are now reminded that it will finally become an armed conflict. Shakespeare also uses the scene to give us a brief, but illuminating sketch of the Triumvirate. Lepidus gets short shrift: he "flatters" and "is flattered" — a detail that will be enlarged on at Act II, Sc. 7, where he is shown as an insignificant character. Caesar extorts tribute, but "loses hearts," as we might expect such a practical but inhuman commander would do. Antony is given fuller treatment. Pompey, whom we may take to be an acute observer, recognizes his greatness — "His soldiership is twice the other twain" — but also develops the theme of Antony's Egyptian delinquence (20-27). This is important at this point in the play. Antony is returning to Rome, and will make a strategic marriage with Caesar's sister, which will seem to end the triumviral faction. So it is important for the audience to remember that he is "the ne'er-lust-wearied Antony," and that Cleopatra joins "witchcraft with beauty, lust with both!" We may well doubt that any attachment can hold him in Rome for long.

ACT II · SCENE 2

Summary

It is at the house of Lepidus, a kind of neutral ground, that Caesar and Antony are to meet to make up their differences and come to some agreement about the conduct of the war. Lepidus entreats Enobarbus to request that Antony go easy with his accusations and demands to Caesar. Enobarbus replies with some scorn, "I shall entreat him/ To answer like himself." When Antony and Caesar appear they seem about to make up their differences and are in the midst of discussing what action each should take against Pompey and the pirates. They seat themselves for the formal conversation which will heal the breach between them. Antony begins on the defensive, saying that Caesar concerns himself with things which are not his business, things which obviously are very much. Caesar defends himself, saying that Antony's being in Egypt has caused Caesar much trouble in Rome, when Antony's duty was to be there to assist him. He accuses Antony of having set his brother against Caesar, which is denied. His brother acted on his own. Caesar further reminds him of the way he treated the Messenger sent to Egypt. He refuses to accept Antony's excuse for this and becomes very heated, setting aside Lepidus' advice to be less harsh. On the questions of arms and assistance, which Caesar says Antony denied him, Antony makes a weak excuse that he merely neglected to send the aid. Antony promises that he will make amends and everyone agrees that this is a noble gesture, with Enobarbus recognizing that if afterwards they wish to forget the compact made now they can do so with ease. Agrippa, one of Caesar's men, makes the bold suggestion that they can ensure the honor of this reconciliation through Antony's marriage to Caesar's sister, Octavia, who is a widow. Antony agrees to this move with little apparent concern for what Cleopatra will do when she hears of the marriage. They shake hands on this and leave it only to Octavia to decide. After a brief review of where they stand in power with respect to Pompey, they go to consult Octavia. The next part of the scene contains one of the most beautiful and famous descriptions in all literature. Enobarbus, Agrippa, and Maecenas remain behind to talk, and the conversation turns inevitably to Egypt and the Queen of the Nile. Enobarbus first describes the life they all led there, and then goes on to give us a vivid and spectacular picture of Cleopatra on her barge on the Nile. The speech, having almost the quality of a set piece for the actor, begins with the words: "The barge she sat in, like a burnished throne,/ Burned on the water." It concludes with Enobarbus' cautionary words that Antony will never leave her, he cannot do so; no one could.

Commentary

This scene has been carefully prepared by all that has gone before. By now we have seen Egypt, we have seen Rome, and we know Antony. Here Antony, having left Egypt and Cleopatra, returns to Rome: this will be a scene of conflict and compromise. It is lengthy, and may best be treated in three parts, 1) the meeting of Antony and Caesar, 2) the arrangement of Antony's marriage to Caesar's sister, Octavia, and 3) Enobarbus' account of Cleopatra, given to Maecenas and Agrippa.

The confrontation of Antony and Caesar is given a dramatic introduction by the preliminary meeting of Lepidus and Enobarbus. Here the ill-concealed contention between the two factions is already apparent. The "flatterer," Lepidus, tries, with soft words, to persuade Enobarbus to make Antony's attitude "soft and gentle." Enobarbus, as we might expect, assumes his customary, rough-hewn, soldierly manner: Antony will answer "like himself," whether Caesar likes it or not. The exchange, and Lepidus' nervousness about the coming meeting, prepares us for the entry of the principals at 14. The debate that follows, between Antony and Caesar, is a wary piece of verbal fencing and jockeying for position. Caesar's desire to show Antony as the offender is obvious, but Antony's defence of his actions (his wife's conniving, and his "poisoned hours") is direct and honest. Maecenas and Lepidus interject remarks intended to heal the breach between the "world sharers," and provoke Enobarbus' acid comments on such face-saving political amenities: Antony and Caesar may "borrow one another's love for the instant," i.e. while they are in trouble, but they will "return it again" when it no longer suits their ambitions. Here, as elsewhere, we may count on Enobarbus for an unsentimental analysis of the situation. Antony, seeing that Enobarbus' cynicism is the last thing that is wanted in such a delicate diplomatic position, orders him to be quiet (109). Caesar relents somewhat, allowing Agrippa, a consummate politician, to suggest a compromise: Antony's marriage to Octavia. It may be helpful at this point to give two other, very different accounts of the Caesar-Antony confrontation. The first is the passage in Plutarch which Shakespeare used as a source for this segment of his play. "For when Antonius landed in Italy, and that men saw Caesar asked nothing of him, and that Antonius on the other side laid all the fault and burden on his wife Fulvia; the friends of both parties would not suffer them to unrip any old matters, and to prove or defend who had the wrong or right, and who was the first procurer of this war, fearing to make matters worse between them, making the sea Ionium the bounds of their division. For they gave all the provinces eastward unto Antonius, and the countries westward unto Caesar, and left Africa unto Lepidus: and made a law, that they three, one after another, should make their friends consuls, when they would not be themselves. This seemed to be a sound counsel, but yet it was to be confirmed with a straighter bond, which fortune offered thus. There was Octavia, the eldest sister of Caesar, not by one mother, for she came of Ancharia, and Caesar himself afterwards of Accia. It is reported, that he dearly loved his sister Octavia, for indeed she was a noble lady, and left the widow of her first husband Caius Marcellus, who died not long before: and it seemed also that Antonius had been widower ever since the death of his wife Fulvia. For he denied not that he kept Cleopatra, so did he not confess that he had her as his wife: and so with reason he did defend the love he bare unto his Egyptian Cleopatra. Thereupon every man did set forward this marriage, hoping thereby that this lady Octavia, having an excellent grace, wisdom, and honesty, joined unto so rare a beauty, when she were with Antonius (he loving her as so worthy a lady deserveth) she should be a good mean to keep good love and amity betwixt her brother and him. So when Caesar and he had made the match between them, they both went to Rome about this marriage, although it was against the law that a widow should be married within ten months after her husband's death. Howbeit the senate dispensed with the law, and so the marriage proceeded accordingly.''

The account given by Plutarch is fairly explicit about the political contrivance of the marriage between Antony and Octavia. Every reader, or director, of the play must decide for himself just how far Shakespeare goes in suggesting this contrivance in the stage version. Traversi, in an acute analysis of the scene, thinks that Antony is as responsible as Caesar for the ''sordid reconciliation'' which the marriage confirms. Antony and Octavius, brought together for an attempted settlement of their differences, first eye one another in mutual distrust like two hard-faced gamesters, each jealous of what he is pleased to regard as his reputation and each equally distrustful of the trick which he feels his fellow ''pillar of the world'' may have up his sleeve, and are finally persuaded by the calculating go-between Agrippa to build a sham agreement on the sacrifice by Caesar of his own helpless sister Octavia. The successive stages of this shameful proceeding are indeed beautifully indicated. To Caesar's frigid greeting, ''Welcome to Rome,'' Antony replies with an equally distant ''thank you,'' and to his further laconic invitation, ''Sit,'' with the corresponding show of wary courtesy: ''Sit, sir.'' These preliminaries over, the true discussion is opened by Antony with a phrase that shows, in its deliberate churlishness, his determination to be the first to take offence: ''you take things ill which are not so, / Or being, concern you not.'' If, after a considerable amount of mutual recrimination, in which Caesar's thin-lipped, efficient disdain and Antony's libertine carelessness display themselves to the worst possible advantage, the trend of the discussion changes, it is because of one of those sudden, theatrical changes of mood for which Antony's behavior is notable throughout. Caesar's accusation or perjury prompts a facile gesture to ''honor'' (85), and this in turn leads to a show of self-excuse which reflects yet another facet of Antony's shifting personality. His oath to come to Caesar's aid has been, in his view, ''neglected'' rather than denied; negligence, indeed, has always been an outstanding feature of this character, and the excuse is, not for the first time, that of the weak man who ascribes his own failing to the machination of others: ''. . . when poison'd hours had bound me up/ From mine own knowledge.'' The ''poison,'' indeed, has worked more deeply than Antony knows. His infatuation for Cleopatra, which he is now turning with singular meanness into an excuse for his own indignity, is at least as much the product as the cause of his self-betrayal.

Having thus shifted the fault, to his own satisfaction, upon Fulvia, upon Cleopatra, upon anyone but himself, Antony's "honor" is satisfied and he is ready to come to terms. Around him are the helpless tool Lepidus, always disposed to find "nobility" in the words of the shabby cutthroats who surround him, and Agrippa, ready as a courtier should always be able to whisper his supremely cynical suggestions into his master's ear: "Thou hast a sister . . . Mark Antony is a widower." Thus seconded, and with the ground so prepared, the most dishonorable project cannot but prevail. It is indeed insinuated before it is openly proposed, and the jibe implied by Agrippa when he describes Antony as a "widower" is sufficient to produce in him, after Caesar's ironic reference to Cleopatra, the parody of "honor" contained in his "I am not married, Caesar": a false dignity which fittingly crowns a false situation and leads to a transaction as cynical as it is clearly destined to be impermanent. The degradation implied in Antony's relationship to the political action which surrounds him will find no expression more complete than this most specious and sordid of reconciliations. This evaluation is certainly not favorable to Antony, and the reader may want to qualify it somewhat by recalling that, during this scene, he shows (or the actor can interpret the lines as showing) considerable sincerity in facing the problem (45-54), is credible in his account of Fulvia's role in it (61-67, 94-8), and apologizes with dignity for his treatment of Caesar's ambassadors (74-98). Another critic, A.C. Bradley, regards the marriage of convenience as the result of Caesar's propensity for plot-making: "Plutarch says that Octavius was reported to love his sister dearly; and Shakespeare's Octavius several times expresses such love. When, then, he proposed the marriage with Antony (for of course it was he who spoke through Agrippa), was he honest, or was he laying a trap and, in doing so, sacrificing his sister? Did he hope the marriage would really unite him with his brother-in-law; or did he merely mean it to be a source of future differences; so did he calculate that, whether it secured peace or dissension, it would in either case bring him great advantage? Shakespeare, who was quite as intelligent as his readers, must have asked himself some such question; but he may not have cared to answer it even to himself . . . If I were forced to choose, I should take the view that Octavius was, at any rate, not wholly honest; partly because I think it best suits Shakespeare's usual way of conceiving a character of that kind; partly because Plutarch construed in this manner Octavius' behavior in regard to his sister at a later time, and this hint might naturally influence the poet's way of imagining his earlier action" (Oxford Lectures on Poetry). The passage from Plutarch that Bradley has in mind concerns a later visit of Octavia to Antony, and runs: "Now while Antony was busy in this preparation, Octavia his wife, whom he had left at Rome, would needs take sea to come unto him. Her brother Octavius Caesar was willing unto it, not for his respect at all (as most authors do report) as for that he might have an honest color to make war with Antonius if he did misuse her, and not esteem of her as she ought to be."

In other words, Shakespeare was dramatizing a complex and ambiguous situation, as the arguments above demonstrate. What is certain is that the marriage is a political stratagem (see Caesar's remark at 114-6), that it is not made for love, and that it will not last. The scene also adds another dimension to the Rome-Egypt contrast. Love in Egypt (Antony-Cleopatra) is passionate and real, though disapproved of by "social morality" and unsanctified by marriage; love in Rome (Antony-Octavia) is emotionally empty, though approved of by "social morality" (Caesar, Agrippa and the rest) and sanctified by marriage.

This has been a long Roman scene, and to redress the balance Shakespeare returns to the Egyptian theme in Enobarbus' famous account of Cleopatra. We may note briefly several aspects of Shakespeare's poetic technique here. 1) The subtle but distinct shift from the preceding prose to poetry, as befits the subject. The uneven prose rhythms give way to a recurrent iambic beat, and the incantatory quality of the poetry is underlined by the alliteration of the opening in the repeated consonant "b" in "barge, burnished, burned, beaten." 2) There is no specific physical description of Cleopatra, in part because a boy-actor is playing the role, but mainly because Shakespeare wants to create the sensuous effect Cleopatra produces, rather than a picture of the woman herself. Thus in 192-6 he evokes the effect of beauty on three of the senses — sight, smell and hearing — to give us the impression of overpowering beauty in general. 3) The whole speech, down to 212, is a kind of verbal re-creation of one of those elaborate, rich, vivid Renaissance paintings with which many of his audience would be familiar, and Shakespeare makes the parallel explicit: his Cleopatra "O'erpicturing that Venus where we see/ The fancy outwork nature." What is remarkable is that Shakespeare follows Plutarch very closely here. Of Cleopatra's appearance in the barge Plutarch writes: ". . . the poop whereof was gold, the sails purple, and the oars of silver, which kept stroke in rowing after the sound of the music of flutes, hautboys, zithers, viols, and such other instruments as they played upon the barge. For the person of herself, she was laid under a pavilion of cloth of gold of tissue, apparelled and attired like the goddess Venus, commonly drawn in picture: and hard by her, on either hand, pretty fair boys apparelled as painters do set forth the god Cupid, with little fans in their hands, with which they fanned wind upon her. Her ladies also, the fairest of them, were apparelled like the nymphs Nereides (which are the mermaids of the waters) and like the Graces; some steering the helm, others tending the tackle and ropes of the barge, out of which there came a wonderful passing sweet savor of perfumes, that perfumed the wharf's side, pestered with innumerable multitudes of people. Some of them followed the barge all along the river's side: others also ran out of the city to see her coming in. So that in the end there ran such a multitude of people one after another to see her, that Antonius was left alone in the market place, in his imperial seat, to give audience: and there went a rumor in the people's mouths that the goddess Venus was come

to play with the god Bacchus, for the general good of all Asia."
Shakespeare's additions and subtractions to this passage are
quantitatively not great, but qualitatively they are the difference between
expository prose and lyrical poetry.

ACT II · SCENE 3

Summary

Antony and Octavia have been married. Antony tells her that his
duty will often call him away from her, and she replies that during such
times she will pray to the gods for him. He apologizes for his past
reputation, promising that in the future he will be responsive to the call
of duty. She leaves with Caesar, and Antony turns to question the
Soothsayer whom we met before in Egypt. The Soothsayer says that in
every confrontation between Caesar and Antony, Caesar's fortunes will
be greater. Antony doesn't want to hear this and dismisses him. After he
has left, Antony recognizes the insight that the Seer has and suddenly
reverses himself on all the oaths he has made to Octavia. He will leave her
and return to Egypt where his pleasure lies.

Commentary

Despite Antony's apologies for the "blemishes" of his former life,
the coldness and formality between him and Octavia does not augur well
for their marriage. The Soothsayer reappears and, as always in Shakespeare's plays, what he says carries a tone of ominous foreboding. The
ill-fortune of Antony when in competition with Caesar is reported by
Plutarch: "The soothsayer told Antonius plainly that his fortune (which
of itself was excellent good, and very great) was altogether blemished and
obscured by Caesar's fortune: and therefore he counselled him utterly to
leave his company, and to get him as far from him as he could. "For thy
demon" said he, (that is to say the good angel or spirit which keepeth
thee) "is afraid of his: and being courageous and high when he is alone,
becometh fearful and timorous when he cometh near unto the other."
Howsoever it was, the events ensuing proved the Egyptian's words true:
for it is said, that as often as they drew cuts for a pastime, or whether
they played at dice, Antonius always lost. Oftentimes when they were
disposed to see a cock-fight, or quails that were taught to fight with one
another, Caesar's cocks or quails did ever overcome."

Scene 4 is simply an appendage to 3, showing the conclusion in the
Roman pact in the preparation for action.

ACT II · SCENE 4

Summary

This is one of many very brief scenes in the play which serves as little
more than a transition. It consists of a conversation among Lepidus,
Maecenas, and Agrippa, who are leaving for the battlefront. Agrippa says
Antony will no sooner kiss his wife good-bye than he will be off to the

battle as well. Lepidus says he has several things to do first, but will meet them in two days.

ACT II · SCENE 5

Summary

The previous scene served as a transition between Rome and Egypt. Now we are once again in the palace of Cleopatra whom we last saw at the end of Act I. The effect of Antony's departure on Cleopatra has been very severe. She has lost all interest in pleasure and cannot make up her mind to any kind of entertainment, such as she used to enjoy when he was with her. First she calls for music; then she wants a game of billiards; then she would be off to fish in the Nile — all the time filling her speech with references to the absent Antony. Her imagination populates the world with a million Antonys. A Messenger enters and she immediately anticipates the worst news, that he is dead. The message he has for her is that Antony is married to Octavia. Cleopatra threatens him with dire consequences if the news he brings is bad news, but she hardly gives him any opportunity to relate his message. When she eventually lets him tell her about the marriage, she nearly faints. In anger she strikes the Messenger who begs her indulgence as only the bringer of the tidings, not the maker of them. She draws a knife to harm him, but he runs away before she can do so. He is persuaded to return in hopes that he will retract his news, but when he cannot she turns in fury against him again. Then, like a true woman, she sends Alexas to enquire of the Messenger the appearance of Octavia.

Commentary

The first 23 lines of this scene, up to the entrance of the Messenger, provide a good example of the way in which Shakespeare transmutes his source-material into dramatic poetry. The fishing incident is taken direct from Plutarch: "On a time Antony went to angle for fish, and when he could take none, he was as angry as could be, because Cleopatra stood by. Wherefore he secretly commanded the fishermen, that when he cast in his line, they should straight dive under the water, and put a fish on his hook which they had taken beforehand: and so snatched up his angling rod, and brought up a fish twice or thrice. Cleopatra found it straight, yet she seemed not to see it, but wondered at his excellent fishing. But when she was alone by herself among her own people, she told them how it was, and bade them next morning be on the water to see the fishing. A number of people came to the haven, and got into the fisher boats to see this fishing. Antonius then threw in his line, and Cleopatra straight commanded one of her men to dive under the water before Antonius' men, and put some old salt-fish upon his bait, like unto those that are brought out of the country of Pont. When he had hung the fish on his hook, Antonius, thinking he had taken a fish indeed, snatched up his line presently. Then they all fell a-laughing. Cleopatra, laughing also, said

39

unto him: "Leave us, my lord, Egyptians (which dwell in the country of Pharus and Canobis) your angling-rod: this is not thy profession: thou must hunt after conquering of realms and countries'." In his account Shakespeare retains the "salt-fish" joke, but what is more important, from the point of view of dramatic poetry, is the imaginative force he gives to the act of fishing, making it represent, or symbolize, a quality in Cleopatra herself. This may become clearer if we think of the way the process of representation through images or symbols works in moving pictures. An image seen momentarily on the screen — it may be of almost anything, a gun, a child's toy, a sunset — may convey a good deal to the audience by way of association: the gun may signify violence, the toy youth, the sunset the end of something. In the short passage in which she describes herself fishing (10-15) Cleopatra evokes just such a significant picture or image, with special connotations. These are, of course, given in the particular words used. Cleopatra, as she sees herself, is not simply a woman fishing. She will "betray" the fishes, and her "bended hook" will "pierce" them, and as she captures them, and cries in triumph, she identifies them with Antony, whom she has "caught." The description has an emphatic note of predatory cruelty: love, for Cleopatra, is not mild affection, but a passionate, and possibly destructive conquest. The image is of the hunt, and Antony is the victim. In this brief re-creation of Plutarch's fishing incident, Shakespeare gives us an imaginative insight into Cleopatra's character.

One of Shakespeare's difficulties with these Egyptian scenes is the lack of action. Until Antony returns there can be very little incident, and what there is takes the form of messages from him. Shakespeare makes up for this lack by giving Cleopatra particularly powerful and vivid speeches. In this scene the incident of the messenger bringing news of Antony's marriage to Octavia is expanded to 96 lines, most of them given to Cleopatra. From 25 to 60, sensing some impending shock, she upbraids him, pleads with him and threatens him, but gives him no chance to speak. Shakespeare deliberately plays the Messenger's announcement in order, first, to make all he can of Cleopatra's mounting rage and apprehension and, second, to heighten the dramatic anticipation of the audience: how, they wonder, will Cleopatra react when she does learn the truth? The reaction is as violent as we might expect, the stage directions being very explicit on the point: she "Strikes him down . . . Strikes him . . . hales him up and down" and finally draws a knife. This is difficult to stage today, since our theatrical tradition, since the nineteenth century, has been one of effeminate and ladylike heroines. Modern productions tend to tone down Cleopatra's physical assault upon the Messenger somewhat, but the violence of her language is still sufficient indication of her searing jealousy.

ACT II · SCENE 6

Summary

After an exchange of hostages to ensure their own personal safety, Pompey and Caesar meet at Misenum to confer on the battle. Pompey seeks to justify his making war on the Triumvirate on the basis of the conspiracy of Brutus and Cassius to overthrow the dictatorship of Julius Caesar, and the death of the Republic. He is now not only the avenger of his father but the restorer of the concept of democratic rule. Antony warns Pompey that, although he outnumbers them on the seas, they have larger land forces than he does. Lepidus, not caring to partake of the squabbling, directs the conversation to the reason for their meeting: how does Pompey react to the offers they have made to him? He has been offered Sicily and Sardinia, in return for which he will rid the seas of pirates and pay a wheat tribute to Rome. He had been ready to accept the offer, but Antony has irritated him. After a few words with Antony, he does agree to the arrangement suggested by Caesar. Pompey begins to needle Antony about his stay in Egypt, reminding him that Julius Caesar had enjoyed the favors of Cleopatra before him. Enobarbus interrupts and halts the hard words. They all leave to begin a round of feasting. Enobarbus and Menas remain behind. After a bit of bantering between them about each being thieves of one kind or another, their talk turns to the unexpected appearance of Antony on the scene. Menas is disturbed to hear that Antony is married to Caesar's sister, because it means that here is a more permanent bond between them, one harder to dissolve. Likewise, Menas is sorry that Pompey has made his peace with the Triumvirate, because Antony is not to be counted upon; he will return to Egypt, not finding the fire in the cold Octavia that he had had in the hot Cleopatra.

Commentary

Although editors introduce the scene as taking place "near Misenum," this is a "Roman" scene since it is a confrontation between "the senators alone of this great world," i.e., the Roman Empire. It is the characters, and the atmosphere they generate that are important, not the geographical location. The account of the meeting in Plutarch is as follows: "Sextus Pompeius at that time kept in Sicilia and so made many an inroad into Italy with a great number of pinnaces and pirates' ships, of the which were captains two notable pirates, Menas and Menecrates, who so scoured all the sea thereabouts that none durst peep out with a sail. Furthermore Sextus Pompeius had dealt very friendly with Antonius, for he had courteously received his mother when she fled out of Italy with Fulvia, and therefore they thought good to make peace with him. So they met all three together by the mount of Misena, upon a hill that runneth far into the sea: Pompey having his ships riding hard by at anchor, and Antonius and Caesar their armies upon the shore-side, directly over against him. Now, after they had agreed that Sextus Pompeius should have Sicilia and Sardinia, with this condition, that he should rid the sea of all thieves and pirates and make it safe for passengers, and withal, that he should send a certain quantity of wheat to Rome, one of them did feast another and drew cuts who should begin. It was Pompeius' chance to invite them first. Whereupon Antonius asked him: "And where shall we sup?" "There," said Pompey, and showed him his admiral galley, which had six banks of oars: "that," said he, "is my father's house they have left me." He spoke it to taunt Antonius, because he had his father's house, that was Pompey the Great." Shakespeare preserves most of this. Pompey "taunts" Antony with the possession of his father's house (27-9), they agree on the Sicily-Sardinia bargain (35), Pompey issues the invitation to banquet on his galley (80), and Enobarbus, blunt as ever, refers directly to Menas' piracy (92). But perhaps the most important thing Shakespeare has taken from Plutarch (where it is only barely suggested) is the threat of potential conflict which hangs over the scene. Pompey threatens directly: "We shall talk before we fight," to which Antony later encounters: "Thou canst not fear us Pompey, with thy sails." Despite the apparent agreement, we are made to feel, as in all these Roman scenes, an undercurrent of intrigue and possible violence, which will become overt later, in the scene on Pompey's galley, and the final falling-out of Antony and Caesar.

As usual in a "Roman" scene there are frequent allusions to Egypt and Cleopatra. Antony's remark about "beds i' th' East" (50) reminds us of the powerful attractions there. Pompey's references to "your fine Egyptian cookery" and Julius Caesar growing "fat with feasting there" (65) are heavily sardonic, and we may imagine Antony's angry reaction. Enobarbus' reference at 70 is to an oft-quoted event, which he takes from Plutarch. When Julius Caesar was in Alexandria he "secretly sent for Cleopatra, who was in the country, to come to him. She, only taking Apollodorus Sicilian of all her friends, took a little boat, and went away with him in it in the night, and came and landed hard by the foot of the castle. Then having no other means to come into the court without being known, she laid herself down upon a mattress of flockbed, which Apollodorus her friend tied and bound together like a bundle with a great leather thong, and so took her upon his back and brought her thus hampered in this fardle unto Caesar at the castle gate. This was the first occasion (as it is reported) that Caesar made to love her: but afterwards, when he saw her sweet conversation and pleasant entertainment, he fell then in further liking with her." Cleopatra dominates the end of the scene as well. What we have suspected is made clear in Menas' remark that "policy . . . made more in the marriage (of Antony and Octavia) than the love of the parties" (115). Enobarbus, the unsentimental realist, predicts that Antony "will to his Egyptian dish again" (123), and we prepare for the disintegration of the insecure alliance between Antony and Caesar.

42

ACT II · SCENE 7

Summary

We are on board Pompey's galley in the waters near Misenum. Caesar, Antony, Pompey, and Ledipus have come here to celebrate their reconciliation. Before they appear, two servants comment on how drunk they have become. As the generals enter, they are talking about Egypt and the strange serpents that inhabit the Nile River. Menas tries to speak to Pompey in private. He obviously has some important communication to make to Pompey, who, being somewhat intoxicated, has little patience for him at the moment. Finally, though, he gets up and steps aside to speak with Menas. Menas has had the idea that Pompey might become the sole ruler of the world, if only he would agree to a bit of treachery which Menas is willing to carry out. With Antony, Caesar and Lepidus all on Pompey's ships, they are at the mercy of Pompey. Menas proposes to cut loose their ship and then slaughter them when they are thus defenseless. The idea appeals to Pompey, but he resists it with the comment that, had Menas done it first and then told him, he would have rewarded him, but now that Pompey knows of it, his honor will not permit him to agree to it. Menas is bitterly hurt by this reply and vows never more to aid Pompey. Lepidus is carried out, dead drunk. The drinking continues and Enobarbus calls for music to which a boy sings a song about "Plumpy Bacchus." After the song, Caesar takes his leave of the company, which then retires for the night.

Commentary

Once more Shakespeare closely follows the facts as they are given in Plutarch, and it is interesting to see how he arranges and qualifies them for dramatic purposes: "Pompey cast anchors enough into the sea to make his galley fast, and then built a bridge of wood to convey them to his galley, from the head of Mount Misena: and there he welcomed them and made them great cheer. Now in the midst of the feast, when they fell to be merry with Antonius's love unto Cleopatra, Menas the pirate came to Pompey, and whispering into his ear said unto him: "Shall I cut the cables of the anchors, and make thee lord not only of Sicilia and Sardinia, but of the whole empire of Rome besides?" Pompey, having paused awhile upon it, at length answered him: "Thou shouldst have done it and never told it to me; but now we must content ourselves with what we have: as for myself, I was never taught to break my faith, nor to be counted a traitor." The other two also did likewise feast in their camp, and then returned into Sicilia." Shakespeare takes two things from Plutarch's account, and builds this scene around them. The first is Plutarch's phrase "made them great cheer." Shakespeare turns the banquet, at least at its end, into something approaching a drunken orgy. The preliminary exchange between the servants setting out the banquet prepared us for this. Shakespeare frequently uses anonymous underlings

43

or servants to comment, as a kind of chorus, on the behavior of the principals in his plays. The opening remark — "their plants are ill-rooted already" — has a double meaning: it refers both to the state of intoxication Pompey's guests have arrived at, and also to the insecurity of positions of some of them as "world-sharers." Ledipus, the weakest member of the Triumvirate, has already succumbed to the "alms-drink." This prepares us for his entry, with Antony, and a comic parody of drunken conversation. Antony, who is still relatively sober, humors Lepidus in his incoherent queries about the serpents, crocodiles and pyramids of Egypt. At 36, Shakespeare introduces a subtle stage device which is ignored by most modern producers, but would have been most effective on the Elizabethan stage. There, and on some modern stages, such as the one at Stratford, Ontario, the theatrical convention of the "aside" is possible. This occurs when an actor, or a group of actors, turn aside from the other characters on the stage and converse by themselves. The audience hears what they say, but it is assumed that the main body of actors do not. This allows the playwright to introduce dialogue that would be impossible on a naturalistic stage, where the assumption is that if an actor on stage speaks loudly enough to be heard in the last row of the audience, then everyone on stage must hear him as well. To see how the "aside" convention works here, we must imagine for ourselves the stage grouping and stage movement. All the actors are roughly stage centre when Menas tries to take Pompey aside (36), and is rebuffed while the main dialogue — Antony's mock-lecture on the crocodile, given to the drunkenly credulous Lepidus — continues. At 52 Menas tries again, and succeeds, and he and Pompey move downstage, toward the audience, and converse in "stage" whispers, comprehensible to the audience but not to the rest of the actors. Antony, still pretending to jest with Lepidus, watches them. This gives his remark at 58 a special or double significance. He is apparently warning Lepidus to keep off the "quick-sands" of indulgence, lest he "sink" into drunkenness (which happens at 87); but he is shrewd enough to suspect the Menas-Pompey conference as being treacherous, so that the "quick-sands" are also those of Roman intrigue. It is a small touch, but it reminds us that beneath the apparent good fellowship lies the danger of betrayal, and prepares us to listen to Menas and Pompey. At 60 Menas and Pompey take over the dialogue and the rest of the revellers, left at stage centre, go on silently mimicking talk while we listen to Menas' proposition and Pompey's rejection of it. The end of this "aside" comes at 79 when, with his parting "Desist, and drink," Pompey rejoins the main group.

This segment of the scene also exhibits the emptiness of Roman "morality" in Pompey's double standard of behavior, according to which he would welcome a treacherous act performed in his interest by one of his henchmen, but could not do it himself because of his "honor." The whole conception of Roman power, righteousness and honor is brought into question in this scene. Not only is there the threat of Pompey's betrayal, but the general carousing has a quality of desperation rather than enjoyment; the revellers, like Menas, want the world "to go on wheels!" (92). Enobarbus' remark about the servant who carries the unconscious Lepidus off "bearing a third part of the world" is heavily ironic in its reference to the kind of men the "world-sharers" are. It is left to Caesar, as one might expect, to "frown at this levity" and, in his customary cold and solemn manner, disperse the guests.

ACT III · SCENE 1

Summary

Act III is chiefly concerned with the breakdown of the reconciliation that occurred in Act II. First there is a falling out between Caesar and Pompey, then between Caesar and Antony, whereupon Antony returns to Egypt. Scene 1 is on a plain in Syria where the Romans have met the Parthians in battle and bested them. Ventidius, in killing the son of the King of Parthia, has accomplished a desired revenge for the death of Marcus Crassus, a member of the first Triumvirate, whom the Parthians had killed. Silius, another Roman, tells Ventidius to follow on the heels of the fleeing Parthians and finish the routing. But Ventidius has had enough of fighting. He says he will write of his victories to Antony in Athens where they will make haste to travel.

Commentary

This is an example of one of those scene changes designed for the rapid transition of the Elizabethan stage, where there was no curtain to come down or scenery to move up, but not for the naturalistic modern stage with its curtain intermission and change of set. On the Elizabethan (and some modern) stage, the drunken revellers of Act II, Sc. 7, reel off through one entrance, while Ventidius and his soldiers bear the dead body in at the other. The irony is unspoken but obvious. Having seen the commanders plotting treachery, drinking, and incapacitating themselves, we now see, in the same glance, the front line soldier (we may imagine the battle-stained uniforms) who is actually supporting imperial Roman rule. The contrast between degeneracy at the top and courage and hardship at the bottom is obvious, and is underlined by Ventidius' words to Silius on the jealousy with which the rulers regard any victory won by their subordinates. Again, Shakespeare takes his suggestion from Plutarch: "Howbeit Ventidius durst not undertake to follow them any further, fearing lest he should have gotten Antonius' displeasure by it ... He confirmed that which was spoken of Antonius and Caesar, to wit, that they were always more fortunate when they made war by their lieutenants than by themselves."

ACT III · SCENE 2

Summary

Agrippa and Enobarbus are engaged in an ironic conversation. Enobarbus belittles Lepidus who has been sick since the feasting. They argue over whom Lepidus loves better, Caesar or Antony. Enobarbus' evaluation of Lepidus is very low. He sees him as a dungbeetle for whom the other two are his dung. The Triumvirate return together with Octavia to make their final parting. Caesar is distressed at the loss of his sister and warns Antony to treat her well. He hears that she may become the source of further differences between the two men, but hopes to avoid such conflict, which would hurt Octavia, torn between a husband and a brother. She speaks to Caesar in his ear, privately, and what she says makes him cry, which Enobarbus remarks is not a fit thing for a soldier to do. Agrippa reminds him that Antony wept at the funeral of Julius Caesar and that this should be indication enough that it is no dishonor for a soldier to weep. Caesar kisses his sister and they all part.

Commentary

This scene serves largely to forward the plot, and Enobarbus at 2-6 keeps the audience abreast of developments. Pompey has gone, his agreements with the triumvirs at least temporarily secure. Antony and Octavia are leaving Rome, and recalling Antony's "i' th' East my pleasure lies" (Act II, Sc. 3, 40) we wonder how long it will be before he is reunited with Cleopatra in Alexandria. The mention of Lepidus brings an interval of comedy as Agrippa and Enobarbus mimic the flatterer in his adulation of his two greater colleagues (6-20). At 23 Antony and Caesar take their farewells. Caesar's speech (24-33) is as prim and formal as ever, but there is a note of distrust in it — his expression of doubt as to whether Octavia will provide "cement" for his alliance with Antony, or a "ram to batter" it reminds us of Bradley's view (see commentary at Act II, Sc. 2) that Caesar may have planned the marriage to disrupt the alliance. Antony is quick to sense this doubt, and reacts sharply to it at 33. His empty, rhetorical phrases of leave-taking at 61-4 do not quite conceal his hostility to Caesar.

ACT III · SCENE 3

Summary

This scene takes up where Act II, Scene 5 left off. The Messenger whom Cleopatra has sent to observe the features of Octavia has returned, but is afraid to come into her presence. His report is very unfavorable to Octavia, and in its exaggeration of her defects is certainly meant to please Cleopatra rather than give the truth. He describes her as shorter than the Queen, of a low voice, without majesty in her gait and more like a statue than a living person. She is also old enough to be a widow and is too full in her face to please. Her eyes are brown and she has a low forehead, all qualities that Cleopatra values poorly.

Commentary

We have noted that this scene takes up the Egyptian development at the point where it was left at the end of Act II, Sc. 5, but as Dover Wilson says, "Dramatically the interval has given Cleopatra time to cool down and above all to bethink her. The Messenger has also learnt wisdom, perhaps in private from Charmian." Cleopatra, as usual, carries the scene, which is a shrewd demonstration by Shakespeare of the way in which a powerful and confident ego can distort evidence to its own liking. The Messenger's information that Octavia is "low-voiced" is immediately interpreted by Cleopatra as meaning that "He cannot like her long." (In *King Lear* a low voice is said to be "an excellent thing in woman"; we may perhaps assume that Cleopatra's voice was not noticeably low.) By 19 Octavia has become "Dull of tongue, and dwarfish." Cleopatra is careful to ensure the right answer to her next question: the line "If e'er thou lookedst on majesty" is delivered to remind the Messenger that he is at the moment looking on the majesty of Egypt, and had better answer accordingly. He has learned his lesson, and quickly assures Cleopatra that Octavia "creeps," which earns him the response at 28: "The fellow has good judgment." Cleopatra has recovered from the shock of Act II, Sc. 5, she is confident of her power over Antony, and we suspect that she has every reason to be so.

ACT III · SCENE 4

Summary

In this scene Antony bids farewell to his wife, Octavia. The place is Athens. Antony is angry that Caesar has broken the pledge they all made with Pompey and begun a war against him. He has further made a public speech in which he spoke ill of Antony, giving Antony very little honor for all that he has done for Rome. Octavia begs Antony not to believe what he has heard of Caesar. She can foresee what the consequences of this falling out between her brother and her husband will mean for her. She will be forced to pray for one and then turn to pray for the other. Antony advises her to turn to the man who will best protect her. As for himself, he has to guard his honor, for it is his life. He grants her permission to act as a go-between in order to reconcile them again, if possible.

Commentary

Here Shakespeare foreshortens the account in Plutarch considerably, according to which Octavia was successful in her peace-making journey to Caesar in Rome, and brings Antony and Caesar together again. Antony then returns to Egypt and there is "a revival of that pestilent plague and mischief of Cleopatra's love." There is a second attempt at engineering a reconciliation by Octavia, which fails. These repetitive and non-dramatic developments Shakespeare leaves out, his real purpose in the scene being to rouse his audience's anticipation of the upcoming struggle between Caesar and Antony, and stress its magnitude — "As if the world should cleave, and that slain men/ Should solder up the rift" (31). Antony's attitude is not particularly compliant. He talks about fancied (or real) insults by Caesar, and the value he places on his "honor," but we cannot help thinking that Octavia's absence and the freedom it will give him to rejoin Cleopatra are also present in his mind.

ACT III · SCENE 5

Summary

In another room in Antony's house at Athens where the previous scene took place, Enobarbus and Eros, a slave of Antony's, are engaged in conversation. They repeat what we learned before, that Caesar and Lepidus have made war on Pompey. We also hear that Caesar, having used Lepidus to gain a victory against Pompey, now denies him any of the glory of the event. Caesar also accused Lepidus of some letters that he had formerly written to Pompey, and has had him arrested and held in confinement. We further hear that Pompey has been murdered by one of Antony's men during a sea battle which Agrippa commanded. Antony is described as now walking in his garden, furious with the officer that killed Pompey.

Commentary

Another brief expository scene. Once more Shakespeare re-arranges the facts in Plutarch. Historically, Lepidus betrayed Caesar in their joint war against Pompey, but his soldiers deserted him and joined Caesar. Lepidus was not "seized" by Caesar, but deprived of his title of Emperor of Africa. However, Shakespeare's version is dramatically better, since it implies a powerful and clever Caesar who will stop at nothing to destroy his rivals.

ACT III · SCENE 6

Summary

This scene assumes a lapse of time during which Antony has returned to Alexandria and to Cleopatra. We know that his return is in disgust of Caesar and had been planned for a long time. Caesar is reporting to Agrippa and Maecenas the news that Antony and Cleopatra have appeared in the market place at Alexandria and proclaimed themselves King and Queen. They have also declared that her son by Julius Caesar, Caesarion, is to be the heir to the Egyptian throne. Caesar wishes to deny that Caesarion is the legitimate son of Julius because he then stands in the way of Caesar's ambition. Antony has also proclaimed his own sons as the "kings"; to Alexander he has given Media, Parthia, and Armenia; and to Ptolemy he has given over the lands of Syria, Cilicia, and Phoenicia. Caesar has tried to turn the Roman people against Antony by telling them the news from Egypt. Caesar agrees to allow

Antony part of Lepidus' confiscated territory but in return he demands a say in the disposal of the land won from Pompey. Maecenas doubts that Antony will agree to this.

Octavia, who left Athens in Scene 5 to try to make peace with her brother, has arrived in Rome and come to see Caesar on behalf of Antony. She has come without the usual pomp and ceremony that is her due and Caesar is angry about this. He asks, knowing the answer, where her husband is now. She thinks he is in Athens, but Caesar knows he has returned to Egypt. He informs her that Antony is making ready to go to war with Caesar and has already enlisted the aid of many kings. She is torn by this dreadful news and Caesar offers what comfort he can, but puts all the blame onto Antony. It is obvious that she did not expect to be betrayed by Antony and is now unwilling to believe it.

Commentary

Caesar's opening speech indicates to us that Antony has returned to Egypt, and also evokes the lavish and voluptuous life which we saw at the play's opening. The "tribunal silvered," the "chairs of gold" and the "unlawful issue" of "their lust" suggest a rich and cloying atmosphere and Caesar's delivery, heavy with thin-lipped disgust, show us the scene through Roman eyes. The list of principalities at 10, 14, 16 and 69-75 are meant to give us the sense of the "wide arch of the ranged empire"; the conflict that is about to begin is not only that of two rivals, but for the whole of the civilized Roman world. Shakespeare follows Plutarch fairly closely here in describing the Roman's anger with Antony: "But yet the greatest cause of their malice unto him was for the division of lands he made amongst his children in the city of Alexandria. And, to confess a truth, it was too arrogant and insolent a part, and done (as a man would say) in derision and contempt of the Romans. For he assembled all the people in the show-place, where young men do exercise themselves, and there, upon a high tribunal silvered he set two chairs of gold, the one for himself and the other for Cleopatra, and lower chairs for his children; then he openly published before the assembly, that first of all he did establish Cleopatra queen of Egypt, of Cyprus, of Lydia, and of lower Syria; and at that time also Caesarion king of the same realms. This Caesarion was supposed to be the son of Julius Caesar, who had left Cleopatra great with child. Secondly, he called the sons he had by her the kings of kings, and gave Alexander for his portion Armenia, Media and Parthia, when he had conquered the country; and unto Ptolemy for his portion Phoenicia, Syria and Cilicia . . . now for Cleopatra, she did not only wear at that time (but at all other times else when she came abroad) the apparel of the goddess Isis, and so gave audience unto all her subjects, as a new Isis."

Antony's return to Cleopatra is dealt with indirectly. Bradley says ". . . the downward turn itself, the fatal step of Antony's return, is shown without the slightest emphasis. Nay, it is not shown, it is only reported; and not a line portrays any inward struggle preceding it." The inward struggle is shown, but later in the play, in Antony's speeches of self-revulsion. Here we see Antony as we did in the play's first speech, denounced by Roman morality: he is "th'adulterous Antony" who "gives his potent regiment to a trull." By this time we see Cleopatra as something more than a "trull," and Roman morality as something less than high-minded ethical propriety. However, Shakespeare keeps varying the point of view; we have seen the splendor of Cleopatra through Enobarbus' speech, and the corruption of Rome on Pompey's barge. Here it is time to re-state the Roman view. Soon the conflict between Egyptian love and Roman duty will occur within Antony himself.

ACT III · SCENE 7

Summary

For the first time in the play we are on the battlefield. We are in Antony's camp near Actium. Cleopatra is telling Enobarbus that she will enter the battle with Antony. Enobarbus is trying to discourage her. He fears that her presence in the battle will unsettle Antony and distract his attention from Caesar. When Antony appears with his companion Canidius, they are talking about the swiftness with which Caesar's fleet has crossed the Ionian Sea and established itself at Toryne, a town near Actium. Cleopatra reprimands Antony for his slowness in making preparations. Antony's strength and greatest skill as a commander rests with his land troops, but because Caesar has given him challenge by sea he is going to accept the challenge. Cleopatra supports this foolish move. Enobarbus tells the company that Antony has offered Caesar an end to the conflict in single fight. Caesar, however, thinks only of success and not of any personal combat with Antony. He has refused the meeting. Enobarbus warns that Antony's ships are not well manned, whereas Caesar's fleet has had much experience in battle against Pompey. Antony's answer, though, is "By sea, by sea!" One can easily read Antony's defeat in the stubbornness with which he insists on the sea battle against all advice. Cleopatra, not being a soldier, does not see the harm her support of Antony's intentions will bring him. A Messenger brings the news that Caesar has successfully taken the town of Toryne, much to Antony's surprise. A soldier appears to plead with Antony that they do not do battle on the sea, but stick to the land where they are strongest and Caesar is weakest. Antony's answer is merely: "Well, well. Away!" His doom is sealed in such remarks. They leave and Canidius and the soldier bemoan the fact that Antony is led by a woman.

Commentary

The knowledge and decisions needed to make war successfully are very different than those needed to make and keep a love. Cleopatra does not understand this fact, and insists that she support her Antony with her own ships, of which she has sixty. As a queen she feels that she has power, but she underestimates her own nerve in battle and the effect her presence will have on Antony, who will be thinking more of protecting her than of defeating the enemy. Enobarbus is a true soldier and understands his master much better than Cleopatra does. His warning for her to stay out of the conflict is a wise one, and his words to her indicate the sexual nature of the disturbance she will cause.

> If we should serve with horse and mares together,
> The horse were merely (-utterly) lost; the mares would bear
> A soldier and his horse.   (lines 11-13)

Her being there will only be the introduction of a second enemy, but in the guise of a friend, and therefore all the more dangerous. She is determined, however, and no amount of sound reasoning will turn her from her aim.

At the next instant we see the same self-defeating stubbornness in Antony. He is well aware that his strength against Caesar is in his land forces, but because his honor as a soldier has been challenged by Caesar, he feels he must accept the challenge and meet Caesar at sea. There are two emotional forces at work here. First, Antony feels the loss of his reputation as a result of his dalliance with Cleopatra and is desperately trying to restore it by accepting the more difficult path to victory. Second, we have to recognize the possible self-destructive intention in this action. He knows that his chances of success are very slim, yet he insists on taking them against the advice of his most trusted and respected general. It is possible that there is a desire to put an end to the conflict at the hands of Caesar. He cannot have forgotten the prediction of the Soothsayer that he will be defeated in all things that they play at together. If he experiences a sense of guilt for the way he has behaved towards the Triumvirate and towards Octavia, and thus towards his own better self-interests, his desire for defeat in battle would be a perfect punishment. Beneath even this level is a probable separation of his energies from his intellectual faculties, the former belonging to Cleopatra and the latter to his soldiership. No man is able to function with such a division in his being.

ACT III · SCENE 8

Summary

On a plain at Actium, Caesar directs his land forces not to provoke a land battle until that at sea is completed. Caesar's remark that "Our fortune lies/ Upon this jump" is a notice that he has set it up so that he will meet Antony where his own strength is at the best.

ACT III · SCENE 9

Summary

Antony directs Enobarbus to take his troops to the side of a neighbouring hill so that they can count the number of Caesar's ships and make their plans accordingly.

ACT III · SCENE 10

Summary

One after another the two armies cross the stage. Then, off stage, is heard the noise of the sea battle, followed by an alarm. Enobarbus reports that there has been a defeat for Antony at sea. His fleet of sixty ships, the Antoniad, with Cleopatra as the admiral, has fled the battle. Scarus, another general, enters to add that Antony, seeing Cleopatra's flight, has himself turned from the battle to fly after her. Canidius, too, has seen the lamentable flight of Cleopatra's galleys and Antony's following after her. He is determined, now that Antony cannot hope to win, to go over to Caesar's side with his troops. Six kings have already done the same, showing him the way. Enobarbus says that he will yet follow Antony, although his reason tells him he should do the same as Canidius.

Commentary

The encounter between Caesar and Antony, being unstageable on an Elizabethan stage, has to be reported on rather than seen. The previous three scenes serve this function. Actually the battle itself is of little visual importance; it is the outcome of it that determines the progress of the play's concluding events. In Scene 8 we are made aware that Caesar is a good interpreter of human nature, at least of Antony's, as well as an excellent general in the field. The following scene shows us the other side of the situation. We see the foolhardy impulsiveness of Antony in accepting the challenge to combat under terms that are obviously unfavorable to himself. Thus even before the débâcle in the next scene we know the outcome of the sea fight. Aside from the impossibility of producing a full-scale sea battle on an Elizabethan stage, the pathos of Cleopatra's sudden departure from the scene and Antony's hurried following — after presented from Enobarbus' point-of-view, produces a greater sense of defeat. Scarus' decision to go over to the enemy adds the finality of defeat to Antony's ambitions. Inherent in Enobarbus' contrary intention of remaining with his master is the knowledge that he will come to the same decision at a later point. His departure and later forgiveness by Antony are two of the most pathetic and moving moments in the entire drama. Cleopatra's flight is totally understandable in terms of her personality. She is very much concerned throughout with the way events affect her personally. She is the principal external cause of the defeat, but Antony's chase after her is a case of moral blindness, not justified by his great love. She was in no apparent danger, Caesar being occupied with fighting Antony. The subsequent events in their relationship must be viewed in the light of this disaster.

ACT III · SCENE 11

Summary

Antony's disappointment with himself becomes the principal cause of his subsequent defeat. He no longer has the will to fight with a winning vigor. He offers his followers a ship full of gold as payment for their aid and advises them to fly from his side. They all say no to this. In what amounts to his only speech in the play he reflects upon his recent actions. He is disgraced, "for indeed I have lost command." Cleopatra and her company enter. Antony, upon seeing her, can only exclaim in shame: "No, no, no, no, no!" He remembers his past glories at Philippi where he won against Cassius and Brutus and compares that time with his fallen state now. Cleopatra almost faints at this memory. But Antony has only an accusation for the queen: "O, whither hast thou led me, Egypt?" She excuses herself by saying that she did not think he would follow. Antony can only feel that she should have known otherwise. The result of the defeat is that he now must humble himself to Caesar. When she cries out, he tells her that for one of her tears it was worth it all; it was a world well lost.

Commentary

The prophecy of the Soothsayer has materialized. Antony has been defeated by Caesar; Antony and Cleopatra together have lost half of the world. After having been on the top of the world in reputation and honor, he has fallen low, in his own eyes as low as possible. At this same moment the attachment to Cleopatra replaces his sense of duty. Instead of turning against her as the cause of his defeat, he turns towards her with open arms and total forgiveness. On one level this is psychologically attributable to his utter loss of reputation. On a deeper level, though, the conflict inside himself has been resolved for him by the process of external events. The sorrow is that he did not make the resolving choice himself, but had it made for him by Caesar. Cleopatra's attachment to him, unlike his to her, was not part of a conflict. He is the only thing of importance for her. There is something very terrifying in the fact that the only way for her to possess him totally was through his ruin as a soldier, and by an undermining of his rational judgment. Certainly, this was not her intention; after all, she had hoped to assist him with her sixty ships. Nevertheless, others were able to see beforehand the inevitable outcome of her misguided attempt at assistance, and had warned both the lovers of this. Love and war do not mix well. Only the classical Greeks were able to successfully put the power of love at the service of war, and this was only because both lovers were men and went to war together on terms of equality. Women are not made for war. Their own being is organized around a life-preserving aim, which is manifested in Cleopatra's flight and fear. Men, perhaps, are less fearful in the face of death, and more comfortable amidst the hostile aggressiveness of warfare. One feels that Antony's superior soldiership would have won the day had Cleopatra not interfered.

For Antony, the defeat means shame, because in the loss of his reason he has also lost his good name, which was his most precious possession.

Egypt, thou knewest too well
My heart was to thy rudder tied by the strings,
And thou shouldst tow me after. O'er my spirit
Thy full supremacy thou knewst, and that
Thy beck might from the bidding of the gods
Command me.

Cleopatra: O, my pardon!

Antony: Now I must
To the young man send humble treaties, dodge
And palter in the shifts of lowness, who
With half the bulk o' the world played as I pleased
Making and marring fortunes. You did know
How much you were my conqueror, and that
My sword, made weak by my affection, would
Obey it on all cause.

Cleopatra: Pardon, pardon!   (lines 61-75)

The pathos of this scene is unbearable. It is tragic to see a man once in control of destiny become the subject of another's ascendancy. The love he feels for Cleopatra is all that he has left in the world and that will not prove to be enough to sustain his life. His offer of comfort to Cleopatra is all the more pitiful because he might have had both her and his honor had she allowed him to follow his reason and if his reason had been free to act in their behalf.

Antony: Fall not a tear, I say. One of them rates
All that is won and lost. Give me a kiss.
Even this repays me.   (lines 77-79)

There is heroism in his resignation and in his compassion for Cleopatra. He might, under the circumstances of possessing an inferior personality, have blamed her for everything and hated her. Instead, he senses her new conflict and loves her all the more for it. The inner conflict has passed from Antony, for whom it is now essentially at an end, to Cleopatra, for whom it is just beginning.

ACT III · SCENE 12

Summary

Antony has sent his old schoolmaster as an ambassador to Caesar to plead his cause. Caesar's general observes that for Antony to have sent such an unimportant person is an indication of how complete Antony's fall has been. His request is that he be allowed to live in Egypt, and if that is too great a request, to be permitted to remain in Athens as a private citizen. For Cleopatra he asks that she be allowed the "Ptolemies for her heirs." Caesar, without a show of emotion, turns down Antony's request and only grants Cleopatra hers if she will drive Antony out of Egypt, or herself take his life. After the Ambassador has left he sends his own Messenger, Thidias, to Egypt to observe what is taking place there, and to try to win Antony away from Cleopatra with her help. He tells Thidias he may offer her anything she asks. He is also to observe how Antony takes his defeat.

Commentary

This little scene is extremely important in revealing how Caesar has reacted to his success. We already know him as a coldly calculating person who will not stop to consider the finer aspects of morality in regard to his own actions. His denial of Antony's humble request is a serious breach of his own honor and is to be compared with the manner in which Antony treats the defection of Enobarbus in Act IV, Scene 5. Neither is Caesar to be trusted in his consideration for Cleopatra. First, his demand that she turn Antony out or kill him is infamous. It smacks of a need for an ultimate revenge against Antony, whom Caesar must feel is really the better man and soldier. Second, there is no reason why he should spare Cleopatra since her sons will later on be a source of trouble for himself. He obviously has something else in mind for which he wishes to put her mind at ease. We learn in the last act that he wants to lead her in triumph and dishonor through the streets of Rome. The purpose of this is to magnify his own triumph. As Shakespeare sees him, he is a brilliant, but ruthless politician who has finally achieved his ambition of attaining dictatorial power. He has not one part of the sensitivity and honor that Antony possesses. Even at Antony's lowest point we still are interested in and respectful of him. His life is not yet at a close. The love relationship between Cleopatra and himself is still waiting for its complete flowering. Now that they are isolated, they can return to the state we found them in at the beginning of the play when they had only thoughts for each other.

ACT III · SCENE 13

Summary

Cleopatra questions Enobarbus about what they should do, and if she is to blame. His answer places the blame on Antony, who permitted his reason to be dominated by his passion. He means, ironically, to blame her for the entire defeat of Antony and his forces. The Ambassador to Caesar has returned with news. Cleopatra, of course, declines to sacrifice Antony for her own safety, and the Ambassador is sent back to Caesar with a challenge for him to meet Antony in single combat. Enobarbus, in an aside, marvels at Antony's loss of reason that he would think that Caesar would stoop to do battle with Antony, knowing the skill Antony has with swords. Thidias arrives with a message for the queen. It says that Caesar knows she only loved Antony out of fear, not true love, and therefore she is blameless. She replies that Antony is a god and that her honor has been conquered, not lost. She says further that she accepts defeat at Caesar's hands and renders him her crown and waits to hear her doom.

Antony and Enobarbus re-enter. Antony orders his servants to have Thidias whipped. He is to be whipped because Antony has found him kissing Cleopatra's hand, done, of course, only out of respect for her. He suddenly turns on Cleopatra and accuses her of being deceitful, as if there had been something other than respect in the scene he came upon. He goes on to remind her that she had once loved Julius Caesar but that, in fact, she has no real passion. The whipped Thidias is brought in and Antony is merciless in trying to embarrass him. He is sent back to Caesar to report what happened to him. Antony feels sorry for himself and again accuses Cleopatra of being cold to him. She recognizes that Antony is not acting like himself, and heaps horrors upon herself if she should ever be what he says she is. His passion being spent, he is reconciled with her and prepares for a second round with Caesar's forces. He still has his land troops and his navy has been reassembled. He calls for one more night of celebration. She reveals that it is her birthday, which since Antony has now recovered himself, she hopes to enjoy. Left alone on stage, Enobarbus expresses his feeling that all Antony's reason has left him and he will look now for some way to leave Antony.

Commentary

An important change has taken place in Antony. His self-confidence has been shaken, if not destroyed. His reactions to the Messenger from Caesar and then to Cleopatra all suggest a man trying desperately to find his lost importance and doing it through the exercise of the little power left him; he is now using power abusively, like Caesar, but unlike his former self. His challenge to Caesar to meet him in single battle is, as Enobarbus clearly sees, a pure fantasy. Caesar will never jeopardize his own position to satisfy the vanity of an opponent. It is certainly vanity that motivates Antony. Caesar may scorn him, but the audience is more likely to feel the pathos of Antony's decline.

His having Thidias whipped is an act of barbarism, totally unjustified by what has taken place. Thidias was only touching or kissing the hand of Cleopatra out of his political respect for her as the ruler of Egypt. She no doubt expected him to treat her thus. Antony, though, uses the scene as an excuse to show his power to Caesar and to show his anger at Cleopatra. That he should throw in her face her relationship with Julius Caesar would be inexcusable did we not understand the terrible situation he is in. He has become subject to emotional whims much like a woman. Thus, for the moment, he behaves in the way Rome has criticized him for acting. In fact, Cleopatra is more true to him now than ever before. She is far from being cold or indifferent.

When Thidias returns after being whipped, we really learn what enraged Antony and made him treat the Messenger from Caesar as if he were Caesar himself.

> Look thou say
> He makes me angry with him; for he seems

> Proud and disdainful, harping on what I am,
> Not what he knew I was.   (lines 172-175)

He is even so out of reason that he tells Thidias that if Caesar is angry with Antony for the beating of his servant, he may beat Antony's bondman whom Caesar has as hostage. We see him here as a man thrashing out at those he thinks are responsible for his downfall, rather than looking inward where the real enemy lies. Cleopatra does not interfere with him when he is in this rage and only speaks when he turns to attack her for being deceitful to him. To this accusation she responds with words that satisfy Antony and calm his rage.

> Ah, dear, if I be so,
> From my cold heart let heaven engender hail,
> And poison it in the source, and the first stone
> Drop in my neck; as it determines, so
> Dissolve my life! The next Caesarion smite!   (lines 194-198)

The sincerity of this curse upon herself is very effective. If indeed she is as cold as Antony says, then let the coldness in herself be the source of her own punishment. This reconciliation with Cleopatra does not restore his better judgment in all respects. He still indulges the fantasy that he can defeat Caesar on land and regain his honor. But his honor is lost forever, or rather has been traded away for something else, better or worse, depending on the point of view one sees it from. From the Roman point of view his honor has been lost for the worst; from the romanticist vantage point it has been let go for something infinitely more worthwhile, the experience of a matchless love.

Even as he prepares for coming battle and steels his soul to fight mercilessly, however, he still feels the pull of Cleopatra's world of luxury.

> Now he'll outstare the lightning. To be furious
> Is to be frighted out of fear, and in that mood
> The dove will peck the estridge. I see still
> A diminution in our captain's brain
> Restores his heart. When valour preys on reason,
> It eats the sword it fights with. I will seek
> Some way to leave him.   (lines 195-201)

These words of Enobarbus sum up the effect that the past scene has had on a devoted follower of Antony, and the dilemma he has placed his followers in by the abandonment of his reason. In some ways Enobarbus' going over to the enemy camp, the effect this has on Antony, and the decency and understanding Antony shows towards him are the most deeply moving events in the play. After a long time of regarding Enobarbus as a clear judge of character, we see him, too, make a serious misjudgment, and we also see an Antony restored to our good estimation through his magnanimity. The saddest and least expected tragedy — the death of Enobarbus of a broken heart — grows inexorably out of his misjudgment of Antony, and ironically out of Antony's show of love.

Yet the mystery remains why he felt he had to go over to Caesar. His own reason has been offended in watching the man he has loved and respected for his qualities of good judgment and bravery. There is nothing that suggests opportunism. He has not played the traitor by divulging information to Caesar. It would appear that his spirit, which throughout has been carried aloft by his ironical view of the world and by his passionate friendship with Antony, has suffered a collapse.

ACT IV · SCENE 1

Summary

Caesar is furious with the treatment that Antony has given Caesar's Messenger. Even more, he is angry that Antony, who no longer has the power to back his threats, should offer them to the man who does have the power. It is this attitude that eventually causes Caesar to disregard Antony's request for peace at the play's conclusion. Maecenas urges Caesar to follow up quickly his advantage and utterly defeat Antony now that he is down. Caesar declares that tomorrow's battle will be the last.

Commentary

What angers Caesar so much about the whipping of his Messenger is not the disregard for the sanctity of the Messenger, but the insult to Caesar that lies behind the whipping. Antony treats Caesar as if Caesar were a child being reprimanded and punished by his father for having done something naughty. Caesar has been fighting to prove that he is not a mere boy but a powerful man, and Antony's ignoring of this sends Caesar into a childlike rage. Caesar may have the power, but he does not have the maturity and wisdom of the older and experienced soldier.

When Antony taunts Caesar he must know the effect it will have on him, that it will harden Caesar against him. This hardness will be instrumental in bringing Antony to the point of suicide. Thus, we must assume that there is a drive towards death already present in the fallen Antony. It is this despair that is so bitter a thing to see in so great a man. It moves the audience to pity him, but it also greatly disturbs us, for our sympathies have been with him from the beginning.

ACT IV · SCENE 2

Summary

The reply from Caesar that he will not fight with Antony man to man forces Antony to prepare for a final battle on the next day. After making this decision to fight, Antony bids farewell to his servants. His leave-taking is so sorrowful that it brings tears to the eyes of all present. Antony's words dwell upon his own passing and the qualities of his followers that by comparison put him to shame. Enobarbus warns him that talking in this manner is not the way to prepare his men for a difficult battle. Antony recovers himself and they all go off to a last supper.

Commentary

Antony is determined to regain his honor, or at the very least, to die honorably.

> Tomorrow, soldier,
> By sea and land I'll fight. Or I will live,
> Or bathe my dying honour in the blood
> Shall make it live again.   (lines 7-10)

In spite of the terrible pathos of his desire, which we know will not end in victory, Antony's honor is restored to him through the effort and through the magnanimity of his mind and soul at this time of crisis. The victory is a purely spiritual one for him, but this makes it all the greater. For Shakespeare, spiritual triumphs over the self are the greatest of all because they are the most difficult to accomplish. All purely material success passes away after more or less time, but a spiritual triumph is a subject for poetry, and poetry lasts. When Antony speaks to his soldiers, his farewell makes them weep. This by itself is enough to indicate that it is not mere self-pity over the loss of an Empire. They weep, and so does the audience because we are in the presence of magnificence defeated by ambition and youthful pride. Caesar would be totally incapable of giving the praise Antony offers his followers.

> I wish I could be made so many men,
> And all of you clapped up together in
> An Antony, that I might do you service
> So good as you have done.   (lines 25—28)

ACT IV · SCENE 3

Summary

This brief scene is a conversation among three soldiers. They discuss the coming day's encounter and agree that if the navy holds up the army will succeed. Music from the festivities reaches them through the air, but they interpret it as a bad omen. They leave the stage to follow in the direction of the music to see where it comes from.

Commentary

Shakespeare instructs the stage director that the music which the soldiers hear should come from beneath the stage. This is reminiscent of the Ghost's voice in *Hamlet*. In the face of the coming battle, the soldiers grow superstitious. They interpret the music of the banquet as something supernatural.

First Soldier: Music i' the air.
Third Soldier: Under the earth.
Fourth Soldier: It signs well, does it not?
Third Soldier: No.
First Soldier: Peace, I say!
                    What should this mean?

Second Soldier: 'Tis the god Hercules, whom Antony loved,
Now leaves him.   (lines 17-24)

It is the third soldier who may be characterized as the superstitious one. His mind is obviously filled with thoughts of death. The reply of the second soldier is a beautiful piece of Shakespearean characterization. The sounds they hear have probably been muted and made sorrowful in feeling by the Egyptian air and therefore they seem to predict something sorrowful to the soldiers. We know that Antony's luck is at an end, which the second soldier symbolizes in his image of the god whom Antony models himself after forsaking him. In Greek mythology this was always the case. Fate, not the gods, determined the lifespan of an individual, and the gods abhorred the realm of death and tried to remain clear of it. They stood by their human worshippers only so long as they were fated to live, but departed when fate decreed the person's life was finished. Thus, the Greeks took the continued ill luck of a person as a sign that the gods had left him because fate had declared the end. Nothing in the play so clearly indicates the outcome of the battle as this image.

ACT IV · SCENE 4

Summary

In preparation for the battle Antony dons his armor. Cleopatra begs to help him dress. An armed Soldier enters to tell Antony that they are all ready for the battle. Trumpets sound and Antony declares to the assembled men that the day is fair. He takes his leave of Cleopatra like a soldier. She reflects that if he and Caesar could settle the issue in single combat Antony would win, but she is pessimistic about the outcome now.

Commentary

In this brief scene Antony tries to put on the attitude of a soldier at the same time he puts on his armor:

Fare thee well, dame, whate'er becomes of me.
This is a soldier's kiss.   (lines 39-40)

I'll leave thee
Now like a man of steel.   (lines 42-43)

This steel, though, is flawed by his past hesitations and past losses. He is to fight from an inferior position, with all the odds against him, in the face of the Soothsayer's warning. The steel will crack as soon as the battle begins.

ACT IV · SCENE 5

Summary

A soldier wishes Antony a successful day. Antony in turn admits that his sea battle with Caesar was a mistake. The soldier informs him

60

that Enobarbus has defected over to the enemy. Antony is struck by the news, but he immediately sends all Enobarbus' treasures after him together with "gentle adieus and greetings."

Commentary

Antony is like a sinking ship; all the rats hurry to leave it. Not only has Enobarbus left, but large numbers of Antony's soldiers have also gone. To Antony, Enobarbus is an honest man who has been corrupted by Antony's fortunes. Antony is unable to blame him for his defection to Caesar, and his past friendship with Antony brings out the generosity and understanding of his master. Enobarbus, though, when he hears of Antony's reaction, will consider himself no better than a fleeing rat, and die of a broken heart. Antony's last word in this scene is a cry of anguish for the lost friend: "Enobarbus!"

ACT IV · SCENE 6

Summary

Caesar sends his general, Agrippa, out to begin the battle. He further instructs a Messenger to tell Agrippa to put in the front ranks those of Antony's men who have come over to Caesar in order to dishearten Antony with their sight. A Soldier of Caesar brings the treasures that Antony has sent to Enobarbus. This unexpected gift so upsets him that he curses himself for his disloyalty. He now feels himself the foulest thing on the earth and looks to die quickly.

Commentary

It is certain that Antony never meant that his kindness to Enobarbus should destroy the man, but it does. Enobarbus cannot help comparing himself with his former master. In the comparison he condemns himself out of his own mouth:

> I am alone the villain of the earth,
> And feel I am so most. O Antony,
> Thou mine of bounty, how wouldst thou have paid
> My better service, when my turpitude
> Thou dost crown with gold! This blows my heart.
>
> (lines 34—38)

The sense of pain is unbearable. His suffering is more than anyone should have to endure. His death of a broken heart may seem pathetic, and it is; but it is also tragic. He has been destroyed by his own actions. The ironic observer of men and events has been punished for aloofness. Even Caesar's own man can only praise Antony for his gift:

> Your emperor
> Continues still a Jove.   (lines 32-33)

ACT IV · SCENE 7

Summary

The next six scenes all concern the battle. At first it seems that Antony might have the victory. In this scene, Agrippa's forces are made to retreat. The wounded Scarus praises Antony's leadership and wishes they had fought this way at the first battle. Eros announces that Caesar is beaten and Antony goes off to complete the routing.

ACT IV · SCENE 8

Summary

Antony sends a messenger to the Queen with the news of victory. He predicts that they will finish the job tomorrow. Cleopatra arrives and in glory they praise each other and look forward to their happiness. Antony also praises Scarus for his bravery and the Queen promises him an armor of gold. They leave together, Antony and Cleopatra, to enjoy a night of celebration.

ACT IV · SCENE 9

Summary

A Sentry and two Watchmen are talking and suddenly hear a man reviling himself and praising Antony. It is Enobarbus. Before the men can reach him, he dies. Far off drums sound the morning, as they carry the body off.

ACT IV · SCENE 10

Summary

Antony and Scarus confer. Caesar has prepared his attack by sea. Antony is ready both by sea and land. They will go to the hill near the city (Alexandria) to watch.

ACT IV · SCENE 11

Summary

Caesar directs his land army to wait for their best advantage or until attacked. Antony has put his best men in his ships.

ACT IV · SCENE 12

Summary

Antony climbs the hill to observe the sea fight. Scarus reveals that the fortune-tellers have been unable to predict a victory for Antony and he is worried. The alarum sounds and the battle takes place. Antony re-enters with the terrible news that his ships have surrendered to Caesar. He declares that he has been betrayed by Cleopatra. Nothing remains for him to do but revenge himself on her. Her appearance on the scene brings his rage against her and he warns her off or he will kill her on the spot. He calls to Hercules to give him the strength to take his own life, but first he must kill Cleopatra.

Commentary

The construction of these six scenes is very interesting. In the first two Antony is victorious and his confidence is restored. At this moment Cleopatra is his queen of love again. He declares that they shall march through the streets of Alexandria in triumph and celebrate with joy.

Then occurs the death of Enobarbus. After this, Antony's fortunes are reversed.

In Scenes 10 and 11 the preparations for the encounter take place in the briefest manner.

Scene 12 brings the long-expected and final defeat. His own fleet has proved unworthy and has defected. Neither he nor Cleopatra were present in the midst of the fight. Nevertheless he blames her for betraying him. He is being unreasonable, but one can understand the utter despair he must feel at the sudden loss when victory seemed so near.

Shakespeare repeats within the play several incidents with the intention of revealing something through the variations in the repetitions. For example, there are the two battles with Caesar, the two scenes with the Soothsayer, the frequent breaks of loyalty, and here (Scene 8) a repetition of the hand-kissing scene in Act III, Scene 13, where Antony had Caesar's messenger, Thidias, whipped for daring to kiss the hand of Cleopatra. At that time Antony was overcome by shame for his defeat at Actium, and he let out his anger on Thidias and Cleopatra. The situation is different now. Victory looks to be within his grasp and he can afford to be generous.

> *Antony*: Behold this man.
> Commend unto his lips they favoring hand.
> Kiss it my warrior! (lines 28-30)

By his past hostility to what he took to be a too-easily bestowed favor of a priceless gift, he showed the value he places in anything coming from Cleopatra. He further shows the possessiveness he feels towards his love. Victory is the most important thing in life to him now. Scarus has almost brought the desired victory and thus nothing is too valuable as a reward to him. The matter of the kiss may seem small, but behind it lies hidden much that is revealing about Antony's psychology.

To the true Roman soldier, honor is the most precious thing he has. As Antony had said before about the meaning of honor: "If I lose mine honor,/ I lose myself." The quality of the individual is measured by the degree of his honor. Enobarbus was as close to Antony as any of Antony's generals and his abandonment of Antony in the final moment of crisis is therefore all the more dishonorable. He had always been somewhat ironic in his estimation of the human being, viewing the typical person with a full awareness of all his weaknesses, but for Antony he had a dedication and loyalty based on the thought that he was the greatest of men alive. Thus, when Antony fell under the power of love and lost his judgment with respect to the rest of life, Enobarbus saw his object of worship fall. The great tragedy for Enobarbus was that he did not see deeply enough into the heart of his friend and see that inside he still possessed the qualities of magnificence that he had had when he was the greatest soldier.

When this is revealed to Enobarbus through Antony's action of sending him his treasure, the world collapsed. He can no longer count on his own judgment to tell him the character of a man. All he can do with his judgment now is to condemn himself. It is this self-condemnation which is so pathetic.

Through the character of Enobarbus, Shakespeare demonstrates the limitations of the intellect in penetrating into the ways of the soul. In everything that has to do with rational judgment, Enobarbus is right, but his sense of irony prevents him from seeing into the heart of the person he loves the most. It is interesting that in his death scene Enobarbus calls on the powers of the moon (i.e. love, Cleopatra, Isis) to witness his confession of disloyalty.

> Be witness to me, O thou moon,
> When men revolted shall upon record
> Bear hateful memory, poor Enobarbus did
> Before thy face repent! (Act IV, Sc. 9, lines 10-13)

After the Egyptian fleet has delivered itself up to Caesar, Antony curses Cleopatra, as if she had been responsible for her navy's defection. The burden of the curse, though, comes from the shame he feels at being bested by a youth. Whenever Antony has expressed his scorn of Caesar he has put it in terms of Caesar's youthfulness as compared with his own years of experience. He does this twice in one speech:

> The hearts
> That spaniel'd me at heels, to whom I gave
> Their wishes, do discandy, melt their sweets
> On blossoming Caesar . . . (Act IV, Sc. 12, lines 23-26)

> The witch shall die.
> To the young Roman boy she hath sold me, and I fall
> Under this plot. (lines 53-55)

The youth of his opponent seems to be what bothers Antony most about Caesar, as if he feared his own more advanced age. The love between Cleopatra and himself is the love of two mature people of the world. It is not the purely sensuous love of Romeo and Juliet; it is a love expressed mainly in words and wit. He must fear, somewhere in the back of his thoughts, that she would betray him for a younger, and now more powerful man. Thus, he fails to see his own true self and understand that it is this self that Cleopatra loves to distraction and with utter loyalty.

ACT IV · SCENE 13

Summary

Cleopatra rushes back to her palace after having been repulsed by Antony in the last scene. She is frantic at his behavior. Charmian calls for them to flee for the monument where they can lock themselves in. She further suggests that Cleopatra send Antony word that she is dead. Cleopatra instructs Mardian to deliver the message of her death to Antony, with the added comment that she dies with his name, "Antony," on her lips, and then return with word of how he took the news.

Commentary

After her rejection by Antony, the most important thing for Cleopatra is to win back his affection. She means to test how serious his rejection is, so she sends a message that she has died with his name as her last words. If he still loves her, he will be in despair and come rushing to her. If he does not love her anymore, he will remain unaffected by the message. She misjudges the mental state he is in and unintentionally brings about his death by the false news of her own death. In this entire matter she acts like an impulsive woman. One can only pity her, for her entire world is on the brink of dissolution.

ACT IV · SCENE 14

Summary

Antony talks with his companion Eros about the passing of his own life and judgment. To his friend he reviles Cleopatra, whom he believes has played him false. In this state the only thing that remains for him is to take his own life. Mardian arrives with the false message from Cleopatra. Antony's reaction to the news is a further determination to die. Guilt now, instead of despair, drives him to this end. He calls to Eros to fulfill his duty and be the agent of his (Antony's) death. Eros swears he cannot do it. Antony pleads with him. Eros takes his sword and instructs Antony to turn his glance aside so he can do it without his seeing the blow. Instead of killing Antony, however, Eros kills himself. This unnecessary death of his companion strikes Antony as a sign of his own cowardice and ignominy. He takes his sword and falls on it himself. But he has not done the job carefully and is only wounded. Two guards enter and he requests them to finish him off, but they both refuse him. Another companion, Diomedes, enters, to discover the wounded Antony. Cleopatra has sent him to tell Antony the truth. She has suddenly had a premonition of what her report might have done to him. Diomedes calls Antony's guard and they carry him to the monument where Cleopatra is hiding.

Commentary

Antony resolves upon suicide when the world has turned completely against him. He has been defeated by Caesar and is at first under the belief that Cleopatra has betrayed him. When he learns that she has not been false to him with Caesar (although she is now being false to Antony in another and more serious way), he realizes that he is defeated from within himself. His judgment has left him. He now looks forward to death happily so that he may catch up with Cleopatra and beg her forgiveness.

> I will o'ertake thee, Cleopatra, and
> Weep for my pardon. So it must be, for now
> All length is torture. Since the torch is out,
> Lie down, and stray no farther.
> ...
> Stay for me.
> Where souls do couch on flowers, we'll hand in hand
> And with our sprightly port make the ghosts gaze. (lines 56-64)

Nothing in the world is any longer beautiful for him. Only the thought of a beautiful afterlife can console him for the many losses he has suffered.

When Eros refuses to be the agent of Antony's death, and instead kills himself, there is a repetition of a similar scene at the end of *Julius Caesar* when Brutus has come to the end of his tether and wishes to die. There, too, several of Brutus' friends refuse him his death, the office finally falling to a former slave, as it does with Eros. But in this case Eros kills himself instead of killing his master. Antony is thus forced to carry out the deed on his own, and it is a terrible irony that he fails at it and only wounds himself. Perhaps this is only a drawing out of Antony's poor luck down to the last moment. He has failed so often during the play that we are not terribly surprised at this failure as well, only we are pained by the sight of the injured man. There would have been something very wrong with the play's structure had there been no reconciliation between Antony and Cleopatra in life. Nevertheless, this cannot have been Shakespeare's sole motive for this pitiful death scene.

Within the confines of the play, Antony's control over his destiny is never restored to him. He is in the hands of fate which decides against him over and over again. This aborted attempt at suicide is just another defeat for him at the hands of fate, which now favors Caesar in all ways. Unlike *Julius Caesar*, this play is not centred around the theme of stoicism. Eros' suicide supplies the representation of that particular Roman idea, leaving Antony to a larger world of conception, a world of passion and love.

ACT IV · SCENE 15

Summary

The scene is the monument where Cleopatra and her handmaidens are in hiding. The body of the near-dead Antony is brought there by Diomedes and the Guards. It is a terrifying moment when she refuses to come down to kiss Antony farewell for fear that she will be captured by Caesar's men. Instead she and her maids pull him up into the monument. She begs to be able to clear her name with him, but he cautions her to make her peace with Caesar. She declares that she will never trust Caesar or anyone near to him. He asks her to forget his end and remember only his greater previous fortunes. When she discovers that he has died, she faints. For her the world is also at an end. It once, when Antony was alive, was the equal of the gods, but now it is nothing. She tells her maid that they will bury his body and then act in the Roman fashion and take their own lives.

Commentary

In his death the circle has come full round. We are again in the world of expansive thoughts and high imagination. The language again soars to metaphorical and imagistic heights. Antony has been restored to his former self. He has returned from the more limited world of Roman honor and reputation to that of Cleopatra, Egypt, and Love. The conflict between the two is resolved.

> *Antony*: Not Caesar's valor hath o'erthrown Antony,
> But Antony's hath triumphed on itself.   (lines 18-19)

The desire to be master of himself has been gained in death. He has gained it, though, not by his suicide, but by his reunion with Cleopatra and the larger world she represents. His final words convince us of his restored and true honor:

> The miserable change now at my end
> Lament nor sorrow at; but please your thoughts
> In feeding them with those my former fortunes,
> Wherein I lived the greatest prince o' the world,
> The noblest; and do now not basely die,
> Now cowardly put off my helmet to
> My countryman — a Roman by a Roman
> Valiantly vanquished. Now my spirit is going.
> I can no more.   (lines 61-69)

Having gained his desire, there is truly no more for him to accomplish in this world, and so his death is a triumph over the world, not a defeat by it.

Cleopatra has throughout the play been fearful of harm coming to her person. She is a Queen, and as such fears the harm the world might do to her. But she is also a woman and this fear is also a part of her deep femininity. This same fear causes her to deny Antony twice.

First, she turns her fleet away from the battle with Caesar and is thus responsible for the loss of the fight. Second, she refuses to put her own life in jeopardy by coming out of the monument to see the dying Antony.

Instead, she has him hauled up to her in a sling, an undoubtedly painful journey for him. On this occasion, however, he does not find fault with her as he did at Actium. He is dying and he has accepted all her weaknesses. His first thoughts are, in fact, that she should ensure her own safety by being humble with Caesar. This is the triumph of his love. When he dies the world is shattered for her:

> The crown o' the earth doth melt. My lord!
> O, withered is the garland of the war,
> The soldier's pole is fall'n! Young boys and girls
> Are level now with men. The odds is gone,
> And there is nothing left remarkable
> Beneath the visiting moon.

(lines 63-68)

But shattered with the world is her own fear of death.

ACT V · SCENE 1

Summary

Dercetas takes to Caesar the sword with which Antony tried to kill himself. He hopes to be rewarded for the news he brings, knowing how much Caesar longs to be rid of Antony. Dercetas was a servant of Antony's. Instead, Caesar is struck by the enormity of the loss of so great a person, and wonders that his dying did not make a greater disturbance in the universe. Agrippa is amazed that they are forced by emotion to mourn the loss of what they most wanted lost. An Egyptian messenger from Cleopatra arrives to ask of Caesar what he wants of her. Caesar tells him to inform Cleopatra that he will soon let her know her fate, but that Caesar is bound to be generous; it is his nature to be so. He then instructs his friend, Proculeius, who (Antony had told Cleopatra) is the only one about Caesar she can trust, to go to the Queen and calm her fears. Caesar is troubled that she may follow Antony's example and kill herself. Caesar means to take her to Rome where her presence will be a constant reminder to all of his triumph over Antony. He calls for Dolabaella to go with Proculeius, but then remembers that he has already sent him on another errand.

Commentary

The praise that Caesar lavishes on his foe, Antony, is genuine. He has feared Antony and wished to be rid of him because of the greatness of the man, with whom he could not successfully compete. With him dead there is no one in the world with whom Caesar might be compared unfavorably. Antony was a man after whom Caesar might have modelled himself had Caesar been less personally ambitious.

There is no one in the play who remains hostile to the end to the qualities and personality of Antony. All succumb to the magnificence and glory of Antony. Some, like Cleopatra, derive their strength from an association with him; some, like Caesar, can personally survive only by denying him a place in the world. The following tributes from Caesar and Agrippa illustrate what even the enemy thought of him.

> *Caesar*: The breaking of so great a thing should make
> A greater crack. The round world
> Should have shook lions into civil streets
> And citizens to their dens. The death of Antony
> Is not a single doom; in the name lay
> A moiety of the world.   (lines 18-23)

> *Dercetas*: . . . that self hand
> Which writ his honor on the acts it did
> Hath, with the courage which the heart did lend it,
> Splitted the heart.   (lines 26-29)

> *Agrippa*: A rarer spirit never
> Did steer humanity; but you gods will give us
> Some faults to make us men.   (lines 40-41)

If we grant that such praise given after the death is less valuable and honest than the same praise would have been if given while Antony was alive, we still must acknowledge the pain it cost these men, especially Caesar, to so credit their opponent. The greatest compliment to Antony, however, comes from Maecenas, one of the pirates serving Caesar, and in its subtle irony it depraises Caesar to his face.

> *Maecenas*: When such a spacious mirror's set before him,
> He needs must see himself.   (lines 43-44)

Maecenas is in some ways the most objective evaluator of Caesar and Antony, for of the latter he could only say:

> His taints and honors
> Waged equal in him.   (line 30)

This, then, is the objective truth about Antony; his weaknesses and his strengths were mixed equally in him. But objective truth is not the entire truth. There is also a subjective truth, and this Cleopatra is the only one able to give, and the person to whom the audience must emotionally respond. If we do not already feel it, the following and concluding scene dwells on this subjective truth.

Caesar is chiefly a political being, concerned with the manipulation and exercise of power. Thus, his feeling for Antony does not interfere with his plans to use Cleopatra as a symbol of his triumph over Antony. As a politician he knows the necessity of dissembling with his opponent. Cleopatra is a valuable prize for him, but only if she lives to adorn his victory celebration in Rome. His plan is to promise her safety and kindness to allay her fears of worse, and then to take her to Rome as a captive. To this end he sends Proculeius to her with assurances. At the same time, though, he has sent Dolabella to make preparations to recapture her in the monument. It is this plan that he momentarily forgets at the end of this scene when he calls for Dolabella. The reason for his forgetting is probably connected with the emotional state he is in as a result of the death of Antony. The better side of his personality would like to forget his plan, but the more politic side immediately reminds him of it.

By not revealing to the audience yet what Caesar has in mind, Shakespeare creates a certain amount of suspense, as well as giving a further example of the carefulness of Caesar's mind. He doesn't even trust his own men enough to tell them his intentions. Caesar, as Shakespeare regards him, is an excellent model of how to succeed in politics, but in the larger world of the imagination he comes off rather poorly. By comparison, Maecenas' more honest appreciation of Antony makes us respect him the more.

ACT V · SCENE 2

Summary

This is the final scene of the play. It is almost exclusively a feminine scene. Its theme is the triumph of the imagination over the material, the celebration of death with love over life with dishonor. It is a triumph of Shakespeare's musical language.

We are inside the monument where Cleopatra and her handmaidens are seeking their safety. Proculeius arrives with greetings from Caesar. Despite the fact that Antony has said she can trust him, Cleopatra acts independently of this advice. Proculeius promises her safety in Caesar's name if she will place herself under his protection. Gallus and his soldiers enter the monument and put her under guard until Caesar can come. Cleopatra quickly draws her dagger but is disarmed by Proculeius. She realizes she has been deceived and calls for death. Her understanding tells her immediately what Caesar has in store for her, and she vows to destroy herself. Dolabella arrives to take charge of her. She tells Dolabella of a dream she has had about Antony and goes on to describe his greatness of nature. She tries to extract from Dolabella the plans Caesar has for her, but he is reluctant to tell. When she states her fears, he agrees that that is what Caesar means to do. Caesar and his company appear in search of her. This is the first time in the play that they have met. Cleopatra kneels to him. Caesar, himself, reassures her that he means her no harm. She turns over her treasure to him. Seleucus, her attendant, is sent off on an errand, Caesar not understanding what it is. Caesar returns her treasure to her, again reassures her falsely, and exits. Dolabella returns and confirms his previous admission of Caesar's true intent.

She dresses herself in her best attire in preparation for her suicide. A man with a basket of figs (Clown) is admitted by a guard. He has brought her a poisonous snake (asp) in this basket. They converse about its terrible bite, and he leaves. Death from its poison is painless, but certain. Ira kisses Cleopatra farewell and suddenly dies. Cleopatra takes the asp and lets it bite her breast, and then applies another to her arm. Her death comes quickly, just before a guard comes rushing in. Charmian follows her mistress in the same way. Caesar has suspected this possibility and Dolabella examines the bodies and discovers the teeth marks of the asp on her arm and the slimy trail of the snake on the floor, and the fig leaves in the basket. Caesar orders that she be buried beside her Antony. He directs that his army shall be present at their funeral and that then they shall all return to Rome.

Commentary

It is particularly interesting that the last act of the play contains two efforts by the main characters to hide their real motives from one another. Caesar tries to hide the fact that he intends to shame Cleopatra in order to enhance his own victory triumph and she tries to hide that she intends to kill herself to prevent this. What is so surprising is that it is Cleopatra who is most successful in her efforts, and not the politician Caesar. This of course, is demanded and justified by the emotional necessities of the story, but it also suggests that a skillful woman can be that one step ahead of the most celebrated living leader. She is fortunate in having Dolabella confirm her suspicions, but her understanding has already told her the truth.

Her conversation with Dolabella is really her final summing up of her belief in Antony. She has had a dream of Antony:

> I dreamt there was an Emperor Antony —
> O, such another sleep, that I might see
> But such another man! (lines 93-95)

The "sleep" she wishes for is a metaphor for death. She sees in her imagination her reunion with her beloved. Death no longer holds any dread for her. She hurries towards it.

> His face was as the heav'ns, and therein stuck
> A sun and moon, which kept their courses and lighted
> The little O, the earth.
> . . . . .
>
> His legs bestrid the ocean: his reared arm
> Crested the world. His voice was propertied
> As all the tuned spheres, and that to friends;
> But when he meant to quail and shake the orb,
> He was as rattling thunder. For his bounty,
> There was no winter in't; an autumn 'twas
> That grew the more by reaping. His delights
> Were dolphin-like: they showed his back above
> The element they lived in. In his livery
> Walked crowns and crownets. Realms and islands were
> As plates dropped from his pockets. (lines 83-112)

In her imagination, Antony was the sun and the moon to her. (History records that she named her two children by Antony Helios [Sun]

71

and Selene [Moon].) Through her love for him, the world was illuminated and made beautiful. In his might he dominated the entire known world and in his person united Rome and Egypt. When he spoke, his voice was as the music of the spheres (i.e. the planets and stars). When he was angry or showed his might, the earth shook in fear. His generosity had no end to it: the more he gave of it, the more there was to it. In his delight and pleasures he was always above them, never subdued by them. Kings and Princes followed in his train and he gave away lands as if they were silver coins. Such a tribute to a human being has rarely been given in any literature, and has never been equalled. The emphasis is on the bounty of the person, not on the power and influence. Generosity and scope of imagination are the qualities that Shakespeare has invested Antony with and it is these qualities that attract both Cleopatra and us to him.

The Clown with the deadly asp who appears so unexpectedly in this last scene is a sign that we are no longer in a world of pure tragedy, but have turned to a world of romance. He is not the typical Shakespearean clown met in *King Lear*, who comments ironically and pointedly on the tragedy of the major character. He is a figure of amusement. His conversation with Cleopatra is filled with wit and jest. In reply to Cleopatra's question if he has the snake she asked for, he says:

> Truly I have him. But I would not be the party that should desire you to touch him, for his biting is immortal. Those that do die of it do seldom or never recover.   (lines 302-305)

To her inquiry of whether the snake will bite her, he answers:

> You must not think I am so simple but I know the Devil himself will not eat a woman. I know that a woman is a dish for the gods, if the Devil dress her not. But truly, these same whoreson devils do the gods great harm in their women; for in every ten that they make, the devil mars five.   (lines 329-334)

Such comic garrulousness at the moment of suicide can only tell us that we are now in the realm of imagination and romance. Tragedy, which is much more severe and austere, is behind us.

In keeping with ancient custom, those nearest to royalty die when the King or Queen dies. In the case of Cleopatra it is her two handmaidens, Iras and Charmian, who follow her into death. Iras dies after kissing her mistress farewell, we are not told of what. Cleopatra's shock at her death refers back to herself:

> Have I the aspic in my lips?   (line 350)

That is, death is already inside her and those that touch her die. She takes courage from the softness and ease of Iras's death.

Charmian's death is much more touching. To the very last she cares for her mistress. Cleopatra has died before her. As Charmian looks down at her she notices something:

> Your crown's awry.

I'll mend it, and then play —   (lines 380-381)

And then she will play with the asp, she would say, but she is interrupted by the Guards' sudden entrance. She quickly applies the snake to her own arm and dies.

Thoughts of political conflict and personal fears are past. Death is a state she looks forward to. Her death is the opportunity for some of the most moving romantic poetry Shakespeare ever wrote.

Give me my robe, put on my crown. I have
Immortal longings in me.   (lines 337-338)
Methinks I hear
Antony call. I see him rouse himself
To praise my noble act.   (lines 340-342)
Husband, I come!   (line 344)
I am fire and air; my other elements
I give to baser life.   (lines 346-347)

She takes the asp out of the basket and applies it to her breast as she would put her baby there to feed it:

Peace, peace!
Dost thou not see my baby at my breast,
That sucks the nurse asleep?   (lines 369-371)

Her imagination changes the deadly asp, whose bite will remove her from a world too limited to accept her spirit freely, into the symbol of womanhood. Such imaginative creations are the essence of high romance. But the political world is still the real world and she dies not a moment too soon. Caesar, suddenly anticipating her suicide, has sent his guards to prevent it.

1 Guard: Where's the Queen?
Charmian: Speak softly, wake her not.
1 Guard: Caesar hath sent —
Charmian: Too slow a messenger.   (lines 382-385)

In this brief exchange the two worlds of romance and political reality clash, with the victory for poetry.

With both Cleopatra and Antony dead, and beyond the control of Caesar, there is nothing left for him to do but bury them and return to Rome to enjoy the power he has wrenched from them. As he was forced at the death of Antony to grant him his overdue respect and honor, so at the death of Cleopatra, Caesar is compelled to show his appreciation of her.

She shall be buried by her Antony.
No grave upon the earth shall clip in it
A pair so famous. High events as these
Strike those that make them; and their story is
No less in pity than his glory which
Brought them to be lamented.   (lines 436-441)

In their death, Caesar finally grants them the union they sought and he tried to deny them. He accepts the responsibility for having brought them to this end, and is perhaps, a bit touched by it.

Structure

Methods of Analyzing Structure

When an artist puts together a work of art he of necessity imposes a certain structure upon it. The nature of this structure differs radically when we speak of the various literary genres. The structure of a novel, play, sonnet, and oration cannot be very profitably compared. There are, to be sure, certain qualities that they hold in common, such as the fact that they usually begin somewhere, go on to the end, and then stop, as Alice in Wonderland said. But this is not *always* true (witness some modern literature). This, though, does not tell us very much concerning the structure of the work. In literature, which is experienced in time, all works must start and end somewhere and, unless these two things coincide, it must also have a middle. On the other hand it matters greatly whether a subject is presented in a novel or a play or a poem. Things that can be revealed in one form are much less free to be dealt with in another form. The form and structure of a work thus become an important facet of which the student should have knowledge. There are a number of ways in which to analyze a work of literary art from the point of view of its structure. We will consider the simplest and most basic methods: analysis and synthesis. Other, more complicated methods, are the province of aesthetic theory and can easily be looked into if the student is interested.

Analysis

The essence of analysis is that the thing to be analyzed is carefully taken apart, and the numerous pieces are individually examined and understood. This process is valuable because it permits the critic to concentrate on each piece in the analysis separately, without the problem of fitting it in with some other piece. Some of the various pieces one should examine seem self-evident. First, the student must have a thorough knowledge of what happens and to whom it happens. No intelligent criticism can go forward with less than this at the start. Since temporal sequence is fundamental to literature, the order of the events is next in importance. It matters a great deal in understanding what one is examining if A first loves B and then B hates A, rather that the reverse (B hates A, then A loves B). Even more simple-sounding is the knowledge that the causes always precede the events and the consequences follow it. Yet reasoning can often confuse the two without its being noticeable to the writer of criticism. Other important things to be noticed in the structure are the rise and fall of the action, the point when a crisis or turning-point occurs, the point at which the conclusion begins, and the probable reasons why certain scenes follow each other. All questions of structure inevitably involve one in questions of an author's intentions and the inner motivations of the characters. Poetry has, in addition to the above-mentioned aspects, structural questions of stanza form, rhyme scheme, and conventional pattern. The analysis of a play ought to begin with an understanding of its act and scene division, proceed to the events of the story, and then move on to the more subtle aspects, taking the most important first. An understanding of structure may often reveal the purpose or meaning of something which the analysis of character or intellectual meaning will leave clouded.

Synthesis

Synthesis invariably comes after analysis. Here the pieces taken apart in the analysis of the work are put together again, using the understanding acquired in the analysis. Instead of dealing mainly in specifics we now are concerned with generalizations. Philosophizing is out of place in analysis, but it is at home in synthesis. In synthesis we look for the "links" that bind the peices together. Usually these links are found in the motivations of the characters. These motivations are the pre-existing unity in the work, since they occur within the character who is himself a unity. One aspect of the motivation will always follow another either by a natural constancy of personality or by contrast due to internal conflict.

At certain times "accident" will provide the links between the parts, but this is rare in Shakespeare, and consistency of character carries the logic of the plot over from one part to the other. In most great literature "accident" plays a very small role in the understanding of structure. In this, literature differs from reality. Another aspect of synthesis derives from the fact that it is a single mind and a single personality which creates the work of art. The creator himself is usually aware beforehand, either consciously, or more likely unconsciously, of a unity of purpose and point of view. Thus, we can look in the beginning for the causes and foreshadowings of later events. A work is not truly understood until it is known factually in its entirety and references forward and backward can be mentally made at will. This, then, becomes one justification for the multiple reading of a piece of literature, for it is only after many re-readings that this real familiarity can be achieved. The last aspect of synthesis to be mentioned is its aesthetic unity. There is usually a continuity of style and language which isolates the particular work from all others. This aesthetic unity comes directly out of the story and characters themselves.

Aesthetic Unity

A work of art can be said to have aesthetic unity if all the various aspects of the piece add together harmoniously, that is, if they do not jar one against the other so that we are uncertain of what the author intended. We must have adequate motivation for the various actions that the characters take. If we do not, we fail to understand what is going on, and why, and the work seems weak to us. Often the motivation is beneath the surface of the characters and has to be searched for. But, when it is found, and if we are correct about it, all the pieces of the

75

analysis will fall into place. It is possible for a great work to be imperfect in this respect, as many critics consider *Hamlet* is, but this is not usually the case. One example of a weak aesthetic unity might be that a scene meant to be tender and sensitive is presented in obvious and trite language. Aesthetic confusion then arises because we are unable to decide the author's intention. Did he mean for us to believe in the sincerity of the characters despite his own inadequacy, or did he mean to indicate by the trite words that the situation was false?

The difficulty in this respect in *Antony and Cleopatra* lies in the frequently exaggerated language. As a result confusion has continually centred upon Cleopatra's character. Is she sincere in her desire for death at the end, or is she really hiding some personal fear of it and a wish to compromise Antony with Caesar? Only a very careful reading will be able to decide this question. In the experience of life we are hardly ever aware of its unity, almost never of any aesthetic unity. We either think about the past and wish it was different, fantasize the future, or we live immediately and actively in the present without such a consideration of unity. Only thus does life seem real. But in literature, if a play were to be as illogical or rambling as real life is, we would be at a loss to evaluate it; we would be likely to say that the play was formless and boring. Our critical judgments demand of art a unity that we do not expect of life. This is another way of distinguishing one from the other. Even when we do not think about the aesthetic unity of a work, we feel it emotionally, and are sensitive to its absence. The development of this sensitivity should be the goal of every maturing student.

Relationship of Parts to Whole

The idea that the whole is something more than the sum of the parts is an old idea, but it is true. The human personality is considerably more than the sum of all the cells that make it up, exactly what "more" no one can really say. One important function of criticism is to try to grasp this larger quality of the whole and to show what relationship the various parts discovered in the analysis have to it. To understand what function a particular scene has in relation to the overall action, or what part the themes play in the total philosophical conception is to be close to knowing the value of the work of art in the history of man. A great piece of writing, for instance, always has a main idea that is, perhaps, nowhere directly expressed; a lesser work rarely has such an idea, or if it does, it is of little consequence as an idea.

As as example of this consideration let us take the classical conception of tragedy. A tragedy always must have a beginning or an introduction. This then moves into a rising action which leads us toward a climax. After the climax the action falls in intensity until the final catastrophe or resolution occurs. When this occurs the play is over. These separate movements of the tragedy reflect in their order something of the way man experiences life in the midst of significant conflict irresolvable by action alone. What is never mentioned in the play, though, is that this formal structure is related to man's psychic experiencing of tragic events. This can be understood only when the formal structure is examined critically. In *Antony and Cleopatra*, for instance, Shakespeare never states explicitly that he is expressing a philosophy which values love above power, but the way the characters relate to the events tells us that he is saying this. If we make the analogy that the structure of a play is the framework or skeleton, on which the flesh of character and meaning is hung, we can better appreciate the importance of comprehending the nature of its structure and the reason for beginning with structure in our discussion of the aspects of the play. This skeleton, in turn, is made up of numerous parts articulated together. Yet the body is unable to move without the flesh and the inner organs, or without the presence of a something larger than the entire body, a mind or intention which instructs it how and where and why to move. Even imperfect bodies are able to move and function, but the ones that we call beautiful, and thus admire, are those in which there is an aesthetic harmony between the many parts and the whole.

Questions and Answers on the Structure of *Antony and Cleopatra*

Question 1.

Describe the relationship between the structure of the play and Antony's conflict between love and duty.

Answer

One of the simplest emotional problems to express through the structure of a play is conflict. The alternations in the personality of the character can be illustrated by an alternation of scenes in which each side of the conflict is allowed to come forward in turn. The central conflict in *Antony and Cleopatra* is Antony's striving to resolve the emotional problem raised by his devotion to Cleopatra and his sense of honor and reputation in relation to Rome. An examination of the first act of the play alone will show how Shakespeare handles the conflict structurally. The play opens with the mention of Rome and Antony's languishing in Egypt in spite of his Roman duties. After only fourteen lines Cleopatra and Antony appear and the interest shifts to them but with this brief comment still in mind. The first words we hear from Cleopatra are about love, the second theme of the play. Antony's commitment to love is quickly stated. The arrival of a Messenger from Rome re-introduced the Roman theme, and the conflict between the two is suddenly before us. The concentration of interest, though, is on love in the first three scenes of the play. Egypt is the setting of all three and the reality of Rome is vague and seemingly distant.

In scene 4 the action swiftly turns to Rome, without any transition, and we hear immediately from Octavius Caesar. Like the opening of the play, the opening of this scene is a criticism of Antony. Thus both worlds of action which form the dramatic poles between which Antony vacillates begin in very much the same way. This Roman scene, however, is fairly brief (97 lines), though its effect is much stronger than its shortness would suggest. Dramatically we have already felt the presence of Rome since the beginning. The function of the scene at Rome is to establish the emotional and dramatic opposites that Rome and Egypt represent. We are also introduced to the third of the three most important characters in the play, having already met Antony and Cleopatra in the first scenes. The action has been set in motion which will ultimately carry us through to the deaths of both Antony and Cleopatra and to the victory of Caesar. All that follows derives out of what we have been acquainted with in these first four scenes. The act is concluded by a return to Egypt where we observe the effect that Antony's return to Rome has had on Cleopatra. The emphasis has shifted very much in favor of Rome and duty. In the twenty scenes of the next two acts we see Cleopatra in only five of them. This imbalance is corrected by Cleopatra's later predominance throughout the entire last act.

There are a total of forty-two scenes in the play. Antony, the most important character in the play, appears in only twenty-two of them. Of these he appears together with Cleopatra eleven times, with Caesar five times, and in the company of neither six times. On the evidence of the statistics alone the drama is seen to be weighted heavily in favor of the love relationship over the power relationship, at least as far as Antony is concerned. Yet more than half of the play is given over to the power struggle itself. What we may glean from this structural analysis, and what can be proved as well by other means, is that the play is deeply concerned with the question of power vs. love, but that with Antony the scales are tipped very much in favor of love. This tells us what we might look for in a searching analysis of the actual content of the structure.

The battle scenes, which in themselves are of little interest and of little importance to the central theme of conflict, are very brief indeed, or are merely reported by a Messenger, or seen from afar. What is shown dramatically is the alternation in Antony of the two sides of the conflict. After the loss of the first battle, Antony returns to Egypt, never to desert it again. Thus the acts of the play may be divided as follows: Act I — Egypt; Acts II and III — Rome; Act IV — Egypt; Act V — Egypt-Rome. Employing the classical concept of tragedy, the play may be further analyzed. Act I consists of an introduction to the characters and Antony's confrontation of the conflict he feels. Act II is his attempt to resolve that conflict by coming to terms with Caesar and accepting his Roman responsibilities. It is the rising towards the crisis. In Act III the crisis occurs and Antony is defeated at Actium by Caesar. Act IV consists of Antony's attempt to resolve the conflict by turning towards Egypt, the other alternative, his final defeat in battle, the catastrophe, and the actual resolution in death. Act V takes up the problem of Cleopatra and becomes a passage past the limits of Tragedy into the realm of imagination and Romance.

Question 2.

How is the relationship between Antony and Cleopatra reflected in the play's structure?

Answer

The first thing to notice in answering this question is that Cleopatra is much more tied to Antony than he is to her. She has no real interest other than Antony, whereas he has always to deal with the call of Rome. Of the sixteen scenes in which she appears in the play, only five of them are without Antony, and an examination of the content of these five will show that he is still present in her thoughts. Antony, on the contrary, has fully one-half of his scenes without Cleopatra. This clearly suggests the profound difference between her feminine devotion to her man, and his conflict between what others call his "feminine" attitude, and his "masculine" devotion to duty and honor. Their relationship can be inferred to have two unequal sides to it, noticed from a structural analysis alone, and subsequently confirmed by internal evidence.

The event which threatens to divide Antony from Cleopatra in a very material sense is his marriage with Octavia. The marriage scene is almost immediately followed by the news reaching Cleopatra and her reaction to it. Again, Shakespeare ensures that we see both sides of a conflict as quickly as possible so that the fullest dramatic effect is achieved. He does this earlier where Egypt and Rome were quickly contrasted in Act I. Likewise, Antony's defeat at Actium is immediately followed by a scene in which he condemns Cleopatra for her flight during the battle.

The death of Antony and his absence from the play during all of Act V might seem like a structural weakness, but it is very much otherwise. While he may not be physically present in Act V, his spiritual presence is felt continuously. Cleopatra's entire behavior is motivated by her deepened love of Antony and by her desire to join him in death. Antony has entered the realm of myth and fancy, but his example remains behind to be contrasted with the nakedness of Caesar's lust for power.

Question 3.

How does Shakespeare join the various parts of the play?

Answer

Shakespeare himself never divided his plays into Acts. This was a feature added at the time of their publication after his death. We cannot, therefore, base anything important about the play on this division into Acts. On the other hand, the scene breaks are his. There is a particular problem in *Antony and Cleopatra* with respect to the formal arrangement of its scenes. The action of the play is divided between scenes in Egypt and scenes in Rome, between domestic scenes on a smaller scale, and scenes of high political importance. The problem arises, then, of how to fit these diverse scenes together so that the play moves along smoothly without our being too aware of dramatic difficulties. Shakespeare, to tell the truth, is not entirely successful in binding the play together in this respect. He partly solves the problem of the differences in scale between Egypt and Rome by ignoring it. That is, even the Roman scenes have a certain physical smallness and closeness about them. The scenes of spectacle that we expect, battles, pageants, celebrations are all merely described instead of being presented. Two examples of this will suffice to explain this: Enobarbus' vivid description of Cleopatra's arrival on her barge to meet Antony, and the sea battle of Actium; both Cleopatra's arrival and the battle occur offstage and are only heard about second-hand. Actually this is a very satisfactory solution to the problem, because they could never be performed with the same sense of reality that Shakespeare's language gives to them. Nevertheless a considerable amount of time is given over to matters that do not interest us very much, such as the scenes with Pompey, the preparations for the two battles, and the several scenes with Antony's and Caesar's soldiers. They have their individual function, but they are considerably weaker than the rest. This fact, plus the more serious fact that this play is Shakespeare's second longest work, make cutting frequent in performance.

The various sections of the play, then, are joined chiefly by the actions of the characters, mainly the actions of Caesar, who forces the others to take counter-actions to the moves he has made. For example, Caesar sends a Messenger to Antony in Scene I. This Messenger is turned aside, but in the following Scene Antony has gone in search of him. Thus the Messenger is the bridge between the two scenes. The message itself forms the bridge between the second and third scenes. The fourth scene follows by contrast. We move from the receiver of the message to the sender, Octavius Caesar. The fifth scene takes us back to Egypt from Rome by way of cause and effect. We see in the fourth scene the cause of the conflict that has risen and in the fifth we see the effect of the conflict on Cleopatra.

There yet remains one piece of introductory material to be dispensed with: the figure of Pompey who has challenged Caesar. He appears for the first time in Scene 6 (Act II, Scene 1). When all this has been accomplished, the introduction to the play is over, and the development of the material can proceed, which it does swiftly with the meeting between Caesar and Antony in the next scene, Act II, Scene 2. the rest of the play continues in very much the same way. The chief method of joining the many scenes is by contrast. If a few scenes have been devoted to the development of the Roman theme, the audience can be sure that they will be followed by scenes in Egypt. Shakespeare also uses the themes to build an internal structure. Even when Antony has returned to Egypt after the unsuccessful battle of Actium, the theme of honor and reputation is still very much on his and the audience's mind. Even in those scenes in which Cleopatra and her theme of love are absent, they are still in the background. For example, during the scenes between Antony and Octavia, the audience is constantly aware that this marriage will upset Cleopatra greatly. We are already anticipating the effects of it on her.

A character like Enobarbus, ironically commenting on the passing action, also serves to bridge the many changes of scene. The audience can count on his presence and his commentary, whether the place is Egypt or Rome, or the battlefield. His mere physical presence joins the otherwise disjointed scenes together.

Shakespeare has to work particularly hard to keep the play together because of its sprawling and rambling structure. The physical world of the play encompasses the entire Mediterranean area, a much greater physical dimension that in any other Shakespearean play. The Elizabethan stage did not permit much scenery, therefore all changes of place had to be accomplished through the use of descriptive language which set the scene. The audience had to keep awake, especially in a play with as many scenes as *Antony and Cleopatra*, to the movement of the action back and forth from place to place.

Question 4.

In what way does the structure of the play derive from the epic nature of the story?

Answer

In one sense only is *Antony and Cleopatra* of epic dimension as a play. A struggle is taking place for the leadership of the Roman Empire. The outcome of this struggle will determine the future fate and history of millions of people. This is the material of epic poetry. In epic literature the story usually unfolds in many, varied scenes each of which contributes its small bit to the total picture. It is in just those parts of the play where this struggle for domination and power is taking place that Shakespeare divides up the action into many scenes. Act II has seven scenes, Act III thirteen, and Act IV fifteen. One result of this is that Shakespeare concentrates more on action in these acts than he does in either of the more intensely personal Acts I and V. Events, which in actuality took weeks to occur, are presented in a few minutes or even seconds on the stage. Time is greatly condensed and localities succeed one another with little or no transition. This all contributes to an increasing tension about the outcome of the events. For the moment the characters have receded somewhat into the background and the events have taken over. In this sense certain parts of the play have an epic quality and it is the structure of the play that points towards this fact.

Characters

Character Sketches

Antony

Antony is one member of the Triumvirate which rules Rome. The other two are Octavius Caesar and Lepidus. Antony is a carry-over from the rule of Julius Caesar and is in competition with Octavius. He is a man with a very strong sense of honor and reputation. Most people consider him the finest soldier and the bravest general in the world. He also has a feeling for luxury and drinking which works against his sense of duty. He falls in love with Cleopatra, the Queen of Egypt, when he goes there after the defeat of Brutus and Cassius. As a result of this love he drops all his responsibilities as a member of the Triumvirate and receives the censure of Octavius and the Roman public. As Shakespeare portrays him, he is a man of great sensitivity and imagination, strong contrasts and vacillations of character, and a steadfast loyalty to his men. We are alternately drawn to him by his magnanimity and imagination and repulsed by his weaknesses, as at Actium. His kindness to Enobarbus, however, finally ties us to him permanently. At the last he makes the choice in favor of love over power.

Cleopatra

Cleopatra is the Queen of Egypt, and, at least in the religious mythology of her country, closely associated with Isis, the goddess of love and the moon. She has been the mistress of Julius Caesar and is now in love with Mark Antony. In reality she is a descendant of the Ptolemys and thus not Egyptian at all. In Shakespeare's play her physical appearance is never described. Her ability to attract and hold men lies in her skilful wit and feminine changeability. She makes Antony feel the center of the world. During the development of the play she undergoes a profound alteration. At the beginning she is much more a sensualist and lover in the physical sense. Her delights are ordinary, but extreme. She experiences many fears with respect to her own self: that Antony does not love her enough, that he will leave her for another woman, etc. By the play's conclusion her sense of life has deepened considerably. Her fears are gone and only her love for Antony, now grown beyond lust, remains to bring her to suicide so she can join him in a better after-world. At all times she is a consummate actress. She often pretends to be offended in order to keep Antony's attention. She exaggerates, out of her powerful imagination, all the emotions which she experiences. At the end she acts a role so skillfully that Caesar does not know or suspect her intention to die, until it is too late.

Caesar

Caesar is another of the three men who rule Rome. His driving ambition is to assume the total power. He manages to eliminate all three who stand in his way, Pompey, Lepidus, and Antony. As a person he is cold and unconcerned with most human passions. As much as he may love his sister Octavia, he is still willing to sell her to Antony if it will bring him Antony's help in subduing Pompey. He remains untouched, until the very end, by the charms of Cleopatra, or by any love, for that matter. His relationship to the world is entirely egocentric and is focused on achieving dictatorial power over the world. We never feel any warmth for him or real appreciation for the goals he seeks. He very obviously envies Antony's reputation and skill and therefore works for his defeat. He is an excellent politician who knows the best way to achieve his ends. For example, he refuses Antony the single combat that Antony requests. He knows he would lose it, and is not taken in by the idea of honor. Thus, in almost all human respects he compares very poorly with either Antony or Enobarbus.

Enobarbus

Enobarbus is Antony's right-hand man, so to speak. He is the best of the generals we meet in the play, and has been a loyal friend to Antony for a long time. He can best be described as an observer of mankind, but all his comments have a cynical touch to them. He greatly regrets the influence Cleopatra has exercised over Antony. His great description of her on her barge on the Nile shows that he is able to appreciate what it is that holds Antony, but he finds it is not to his taste. Yet this cynicism masks a much finer and more human feeling. When under the stress of Antony's repeated failures he abandons him and goes over to Caesar, Antony forgives him as an old friend whom he cannot blame for his action. In the face of such fineness of feeling, Enobarbus condemns himself for being a vile forsaker of friends and dies out of remorse. It is this sensitivity of feeling that is hidden and protected by his cynical and ironic observations.

Charmian

Charmian is Cleopatra's number one handmaiden, but she is not entirely without her own distinct personality. Unlike the more spiritually developed Cleopatra, she is restricted in her character to the purely physical side of love; but there is a good deal of joy and zest in her devotion to it. She is totally tied to her mistress and dies when she dies. She has a very lively tongue which she frequently employs in a running banter with whomever she can. At the same time, Shakespeare gives her a few added moments which are particularly characteristic and wonderful such as the second of time she takes to straighten the dead Cleopatra's crown before she lets the asp bite herself. She seems to share Cleopatra's enthusiasm for Antony without ever over-stepping her place. She is one of Shakespeare's most entertaining characters.

Methods of Analyzing Characters

1. Describing the Characters

The starting point for understanding the characters should be a general description of who and what they are. If Shakespeare (or any other author) makes a physical description of a character this is a good a place as any for the student to begin his understanding of the person. It helps in bringing the person alive if the student knows how the author pictures him. Is he tall or short, dark or light in complexion, has he a particular and obvious feature or defect that might influence his psychological behavior. The reader may not know what the author intends to make of the character's features as he goes along, but knowing what they are will become important as their meaning becomes clearer. Then, the student should be aware of the person's temperament, and the various sides of his personality, if there are more than one. This will help the student to both anticipate possible developments in the character and understand his reactions to events as they occur. Beyond this, what characters have to say about each other is significant. It not only reveals something about the person described but also something about the person doing the describing. Some of Shakespeare's characters are left partially incomplete: that is, they are not fully characterized. This fact has its importance and should be observed and explained by the student. Why, for instance, does Octavia remain so blank as a person? Obviously, Shakespeare could have filled out her portrait, if he wanted to do so. Thus, a very general survey of a character's emotional and physical being is the best place to begin an understanding of that character.

2. Analysis of Character Development

In the greatest works of literature, the central characters frequently undergo major developments in their emotional attitudes and intellectual understandings. These developments are brought about by the effect that events have upon the person's pre-existing character. In *Antony and Cleopatra* both title characters undergo a significant development of their personalities, whereas Caesar remains pretty much constant throughout. It is important, then, to recognize the nature of and the reasons for the changes that occur, as well as the meaning of a character's failing to develop in the face of major events.

Often the most important emotions and motivations of a person lie beneath the surface and are not immediately obvious. It takes the events that happen to the person to bring out these hidden facets of his personality. The student should watch for such revelations of the inner being of a character. At the same time, there are some facets that never emerge and can only be guessed at, by trying to explain what might have motivated the character to act in the way he did. This is a particularly difficult thing to do successfully, because the characters of literature are not real people in the same sense that the student himself is real. When we read beyond what is explicitly stated we are actually studying the mind of the author.

An important part of the analysis of a character is the critical evaluation of the character himself. Do his actions seem reasonable and "normal" or are they strange and "abnormal"? If they are the latter, is this because of something inherent in the character or can it be traced to changes in society's behavior between the period of the work's compostion and today? The student ought to refrain from judging a character on too limited and personal a basis, and try to understand him in the context of the play. In this way the inner meaning of the play will become more evident and will not be confused with the reader's opinions of the play.

3. Motivation

Very little concerning the meaning of *Antony and Cleopatra* can be grasped without an understanding of the motivation of the main characters. Why does Antony first reject Caesar's Messenger and then go in search of him? Why does he marry Octavia and then desert her to return to Egypt? Why does he whip Thidias and challenge Caesar to do the same with the hostage Caesar has? Why does Cleopatra pretend to be dead? Why does she dress in her best attire just before she dies? The deeper the student understands the motivation in these and other instances, the deeper he will understand the play and Shakespeare. In the realm of psychology and character motivation, Shakespeare is very "modern," that is, his characters act in a way and for reasons that will seem familiar and right to today's audience. At any point where there seems to be an absence of motivation, except in the very difficult case of Iago in *Othello*, about which there is considerable debate, the student should study the action and the words of the play carefully, because human beings do not act without a reason. The real problem occurs when the motivation is not known to the character himself. The most natural thing is for a character to act out of a multiplicity of motives. No one reason can be given for a particular act, because many different reasons go to make up the actual motivation. Usually the action is "over-determined," that is, there are more than enough reasons for action. This is, though, the natural way humans act and we can expect to find Shakespeare's characters behaving in this way as well.

4. Thematic Characters

A thematic character is one who in himself embodies one of the themes of the play. He may be a distillation and symbolic representation of the theme. For instance, it might be said that Enobarbus is a thematic character in that he stands for loyalty. Sometimes a character is only a thematic character part of the time and at certain places in the play. In the early parts of the play, Cleopatra is such a character insofar as she symbolizes the theme of love. Usually, though, a central character is related to many of the play's themes and cannot be assigned to one particular one. The idea of thematic characters is useful if employed carefully and with discretion. The student must remember that a more intimate understanding of the person should be sought than can be achieved by exclusively applying the idea of thematic characters.

5. Analyzing Character Relationships

It is, of course, impossible to have analyzed a character without having seen him in his relationships with the other characters of the play. These relationships are the core of the play; no dramatic work is really possible without them. The interrelationships between Antony and Cleopatra are fairly subtle because they encompass so much of the experience of life. To separate out the various aspects of their love for each other will take the student into all the other aspects of the play. Thus, this is a particularly good place to begin. It would also be instructive for the student to compare Antony's relationship to Caesar with his relationship to Cleopatra. Antony is, as it were, the hub of a wheel, around the perimeter of which are the other characters. Spokes bind Antony with each of the people on the perimeter. Cleopatra, for instance, does not meet Caesar until the very last scene of the play, and has very little relationship to him. This occurs only after Antony has been removed from the center and transported into the realm of the spirit and the imagination. Caesar's actions against Antony are very much concerned with this displacing of Antony and the substitution of himself in Antony's place at the hub. Thus, the interrelations of one character with another can act as a key into the heart of the play, and the student should always give his attention to them.

Questions and Answers on the Characters of *Antony and Cleopatra*

Question 5.

Discuss the development of Antony as a character. How is the conflict he experiences finally resolved?

Answer

The events of the play have a profound effect upon Antony. They cause his character to undergo a number of changes and a final development at the moment of his death. When we meet him for the first time, his is the consort of the Queen in Egypt, having replaced Julius Caesar, his best friend, in this capacity. He is shown to be a man of integrity and deep feeling. He has a robust masculinity mixed with a love of entertainment and a lack of responsibility.

> *Cleopatra*: If it be love indeed, tell me how much.
>
> *Antony*: There's beggary in the love that can be reckoned.
>
> *Cleopatra*: I'll set a bourn how far to be beloved.
>
> *Antony*: Then must thou needs find out new heaven, new earth.　　(Act I, Sc. 1, lines 14-17)
>
> *Antony*: The nobleness of life
> Is to do thus (*embracing her*) when such a mutual pair

And such a twain can do't, in which I bind,
On pain of punishment, the world to weet
We stand up peerless. (Act I, Sc. 1, lines 41-46)

In the two quotations above we see the extent to which he has given himself over to love. The actions which follow from this, his initial rejection of Caesar's Messenger, his long period of languishing in Egypt, and his ignoring of his Roman responsibilities, are the basis on which he is accused of having been made a woman by Cleopatra. Thus, the first side of Antony that we see is his "feminine" side, that which is devoted to love and to Cleopatra. The problem to be understood is that this is his strong side, and not his weak one as it is accused of being by all Rome, and by many readers. This devotion to love is, itself, a major change in his character, because his entire youthful life before the play opens had been devoted to the game of power. Now it is Caesar who pursues that power.

The first major change in Antony within the play comes with the arrival of Caesar's Messenger with the news that Pompey has attacked Rome. His sense of responsibility to his political position, his honor, and his reputation as the greatest soldier in the world are all revived in him by Caesar's message. As a result, a conflict ensues in his character between love and duty which is not resolved until the very end of his life. The remaining changes in him are more, though, than mere vacillations in his will. They are stages in his development as a personality. In the process of this development he realizes the futility of power and ambition and his desire to protect his good name, and comes to accept the fact that he values his love for Cleopatra more than all else. Before this happens, though, he has to go through a number of terrible trials. Defeat in war and constancy in love are two of the trials he has to experience. In the process he loses his sense of balance and his reason seems to depart. He knows that his military strength is in his land soldiers, but because challenged by Caesar he fights with him at sea. His flight after Cleopatra's fleeing ships is his lowest point. By this action he is personally responsible for the loss of many of his ships and men. His faithfulness to Cleopatra is shaken badly and he accuses her of being answerable for his own defeat. Again, at the second battle, he is defeated because the Egyptians surrender to Caesar. This time, too, he doubts her love and is very harsh with her, even to the point of desiring to kill her. But these two defeats have in reality been caused by his own lack of rational planning. He has acted too emotionally rather than thoughtfully and intelligently. But then the final change occurs, for which these sufferings have all been preparatory. He tries to kill himself and fails even at that. He is taken to the monument where Cleopatra is in hiding. She refuses to put herself in danger to see him and he has to be hauled up to her on a rope. This time the conflict in him is over and he has not a strong word against his beloved. All he wishes to do is to kiss her for the last time and then die. It is the final realization that the entire world of power is not worth that one kiss of Cleopatra's is what marks this final development. He has been moving towards this realization throughout the play and been struggling against it, or at least struggling to maintain his Roman honor and reputation at the same time, which was impossible.

Question 6.

In terms of character portrayal and importance, do the men dominate or do the women? Discuss.

Answer

The title of the play would suggest that there is an equality of importance between Antony and Cleopatra. And this is so in certain respects. At the same time, however, Antony appears more frequently than does Cleopatra, and is the only major character to live in both worlds of the play, Egypt and Rome. The central conflict of the play is a masculine conflict between the two greatest forces that can influence a man: love and power. In this very important sense the masculine element of life dominates the play. More that one half of the time is devoted to the theme of power, and the figure of Caesar is concerned with this theme alone. In terms of worldly success the side of power wins out, or so it would appear. Caesar has defeated Antony and rules the world alone. This victory, though, is not the significant one from Shakespeare's point of view. He is much more involved with the theme of personal love, and it is Cleopatra and Egypt who embody this theme. In this sense, then, the women might seem to dominate the play. Even when the only important woman in the play, Cleopatra, is not on the stage, her presence is felt, her spirit is in the air, and her name is on the lips of the major male characters. When Antony abandons Cleopatra, he still has to deal with women, this time in the person of Caesar's sister, Octavia. He cannot seem to escape from them into a purely masculine world of struggle for power as has Caesar.

Where, then, does the balance of the play lie? For Shakespeare it lies in the realm of the imagination and the spirit. If this is thought of as being feminine, as it is by many critics, then the balance is tipped decidedly in favor of the women, who represent this aspect of life. If this quality of poetry and imagination is thought to be also the property of men, in fact the proper goal of the wisest men, then there is a natural balance between the two sexual elements, neither dominating the other. The play makes is strongest appeal and effect if the second point of view is accepted. Only in this way does the end of the play achieve its full richness of thought, its most true Shakespearean meaning.

Question 7.

Discuss the character of Enobarbus. What function does he have in the play?

Answer

Enobarbus is the most interesting of the secondary characters in *Antony and Cleopatra*. Like Antony, he is a soldier, the most intelligent in Antony's service. He is also the closest male friend of Antony, one who has received special recognition and friendship from Antony. His observations of people and on the progress of events are particularly acute, even though they are always given in an ironic and sometimes cynical manner. Loyalty to Antony is his personal mark of distinction. He values this loyalty very highly. In the name of this loyalty he looks after Antony's affairs and is rather critical of Antony's being under the influence of a woman. In the following example his ironic description of Cleopatra's acting abilities is not only perceptive, but devastating.

> *Enobarbus*: Cleopatra, catching but the least noise of this, dies instantly. I have seen her die twenty times upon far poorer moment. I do think there is mettle in death, which commits some loving act upon her, she hath such a celerity in dying.
>
> (Act I, Sc. 2, lines 156-160)

In his opinion Antony is the noblest man in the world, compared to whom Caesar is but a boy. He would like nothing better than for Antony to return to his responsibilities in Rome. He has very little understanding or use for romance; his mind is very clear in its evaluation of things political. He tries to persuade Cleopatra not to join her lover in the battle of Actium. He knows that if she does it will distract Antony and bring ruin. The outcome of the battle proves him to have been right in the exact detail. When Antony unthinkingly challenges Caesar to single combat, Enobarbus sees immediately the impossibility of it and the loss of reason Antony must have suffered in imagining such a thing possible.

> Yes, like enough high-battled Caesar will
> Unstate his happiness and be staged to the show
> Against a sworder! I see men's judgements are
> A parcel of their fortunes, and things outward
> Do draw the inward quality after them
> To suffer all alike. That he should dream,
> Knowing all measures, the full Caesar will
> Answer the emptiness! Caesar, thou hast subdued
> His judgement too. (Act III, Sc. 13, lines 34-43)

It is this loss of judgment that finally convinces him to leave Antony and go over to Caesar. It is a very difficult decision for Enobarbus to make, and to his later regret it turns out to have been the wrong one. After his defection, Antony proves the more noble and loyal by sending him his treasures which he had left behind. The shame he experiences at having misjudged Antony causes him to die of grief and humiliation.

One of his principal functions in the play is to serve as the source of a kind of ironic and objective commentary upon the action. His criticism of Antony is similar to that of Caesar, but we accept it better from Enobarbus because we know he makes it out of his love for Antony, not out of envy as Caesar does. His failure is a failure of vision. He cannot understand the significance of Cleopatra and love to Antony; his vision is limited to the world of practical matters. Within this world of power he is a likeable and respectable human being in contrast to the cold and ambitious Caesar. He serves another more important function. It is connected directly with his failure of loyalty to Antony. This loyalty has been the chief guiding force of his life, and when he turns away from it, he is turning away from himself. The result of this is an utter despair that causes his death. Shakespeare contrasts this with a similar situation in Antony. At the center of Antony's being is his love of Cleopatra. The struggle he experiences in the play is to remain loyal to her and to his love. The important difference between Antony and Enobarbus is that Antony does in the end accept this love and his own death is heroic and glorious, whereas Enobarbus' death is pathetic. Shakespeare uses this contrast to heighten the effect of Antony's final choice. We value it all the more highly just having seen Enobarbus' spiritual failure in a similar choice.

Question 8.

Describe the relationship between Cleopatra and Charmian. Between Cleopatra and Octavia.

Answer

Charmian is the handmaiden to Cleopatra. As such she has a special intimacy with her mistress, but there is also a very special love for Cleopatra. Both women are devoted to the service of love, to the goddess Isis, of whom Cleopatra is an earthly incarnation. In the beginning of the play love means much the same to both women: the physical enjoyment of contact with and protection by men. Cleopatra is on a rather higher level than Charmian because of her wit and versatility in experiencing and expressing the nature of love. Charmian is much more given to the bawdy side of love, to being clever rather than rich in understanding. She is somewhat superstitious, as her request of the Soothsayer for her fortune witnesses. When she and Cleopatra compare notes on how to hold a man she appears to be less knowledgeable than Cleopatra. Charmian never appears in a scene without Cleopatra. This indicates the closeness of her tie to her mistress. She is an extension of Cleopatra. When Cleopatra dies in the last scene, she dies with her. She has no separate identity away from Cleopatra. For her mistress, though, Charmian is someone to talk intimately with about the fears she has. Charmian gives Cleopatra support and on occasion instructive criticism, but not of the firm, harsh variety that Enobarbus gives Antony.

The relationship between Cleopatra and Octavia is quite different. The two women never meet each other, but both are sensitive about the other. Cleopatra knows that Antony, in loving her, has been unfaithful to his wife, Fulvia. She uses this example as a reason for believing that she will be deserted when she hears of his marriage to Octavia. At the same time she also reacts in another very feminine way. She sends an observer to see Octavia and report back what sort of woman she is. On the basis of the report she judges herself the better and more attractive woman whom Antony must then, of course, continue to love. But this rationalization does not really alleviate her fears. The two women are individually symbols for Egypt and Rome. Octavia is really only a pawn which Caesar uses to hold Antony to him, but it is unsuccessful because Octavia cannot give Antony the deep experience of life and love that Cleopatra can. Octavia is too Roman, too much like Caesar. Thus she is really no competition for Cleopatra. Nevertheless, when it is time for Cleopatra to sue for Caesar's favor, one thing that deters her is the thought of the pleasure it would give Octavia to see her in the streets of Rome as a prisoner on exhibition. She cannot abide such a thought. In one sense they are opposites: Cleopatra is the fullest expression of love and Octavia is a woman in whom we see little of this emotion. Like her brother she is generally cool in love.

Question 9.

In what sense are Antony and Caesar opposites? In what sense are they the youthful and mature versions of a single ideal?

Answer

Caesar is much more important to the play *Antony and Cleopatra* than just as the worldly source of Antony's conflict. He is there as a contrast to the figure of Antony, a contrast in the extreme. Caesar is a singularly ambitious person. He is willing to sacrifice all he has to achieve his end of supreme power over the Roman Empire. To this end he defeats Antony in two battles, having already removed Lepidus from the Triumvirate on apparently false charges, and sold his beloved sister to Antony. Throughout the play we see no warmth or feeling for people in him that does not have its origin and its end in his struggle for power. He is a very capable general, although not as fine as Antony, but in political matters he has no equal. He is a man without conflicts. This cannot be said of his opponent who suffers under the most severe conflict, that between love and duty to the Empire. In the play Caesar has no real friends in the same sense that Antony has. No one seems to love him. Respect is as far as people can go with him. Antony, on the contrary, is imbued with a warmth and sensitivity that immediately attracts people to him. Loyalty to him is based on something deeper than material gain. It comes from the response Antony gives to friendship.

If, as many philosophers agree, struggle is the natural condition of man, and the prelude to greatness, then Caesar has to be seen as very deficient in this quality of humanity. His qualities are those of a military leader. When Antony's general Alexas goes over to Caesar's camp, Caesar has him hanged. Caesar is unable to trust defectors, perhaps correctly in terms of politics, but his action is inhuman. In contrast Antony sends Enobarbus' possessions after him when he goes over to Caesar. The contrast in the two men in similar situations is very revealing of their basic personality differences. Ultimately, Antony chooses the side of love and imagination over the power which is Caesar's choice. In this choice Antony saves his soul and becomes an immortal figure of legend, while Caesar is remembered only in the history of books as a dictator of men. Shakespeare's point is obviously to ask what is the value of all the power in the world if one sells his soul (humanity) to obtain it. In their speech their differences are also apparent. Antony has a gift of language almost the equal of Cleopatra. His words express the inner Antony as well as the outer personality. Caesar, if we were to judge from his language, has only an outer personality. We learn little of what goes on inside his mind. Both men are capable of being stirred to anger, but Antony is quick to understand and forgive, whereas we really don't see this quality in Caesar. The most important difference is that Antony is bound to people, he lives life to the fullest through his human contacts, either in love or in friendship. Caesar is withdrawn from people. He basically does not trust them. They are seen chiefly as competitors. He uses them for his own ends, and thus probably does not trust them because he fears they will do the same with him.

There is, however, another way of understanding their relationship to each other. If we set aside for the moment the fact that Caesar has not the scope of imagination that Antony does, it is possible to see them as being different stages in the development of a single ideal. We must remember that in comparison with Antony, Caesar is a youth and inexperienced in the variety of the world. The ideal is the natural development of a man. Caesar is then the youthful stage of this development. He is like all rebels, out to mold the world to his liking, insensitive to those around them. He is very envious of the older and more respected generation (Antony), and seeks to supplant it. He is unaware of his own limitations and judges everyone by his own ambitions. These are all the hallmarks of the young in years. Antony is more mature in age and experience. He has seen more of the world of men and learned the hollowness of the drive for power. When he engages with Caesar it is not power that he wants, but the restoration of his good name and his honor. The conflict he experiences is perfectly natural for someone in transition from youthful ambition to mature understanding. He ultimately gives up the pursuit of honor and accepts the nobler devotion to love.

This transition is for Shakespeare the one every true human being should make. The world of the spirit is more valuable and honorable than the pursuit of power over men, because it entails a triumph over oneself. It is a greater triumph because it is more difficult to achieve and because the end result gives expression to the fullest expansiveness of the human personality. When we remember that Antony, too, pursued power when he was younger, we can properly value his development as that of an ideal man. Caesar, we feel, will never reach the heights that Antony does. He doesn't seem to have it in him to do so. It is also probable that defeat in the struggle for power is needed before the emptiness of its pursuit can be realized. Caesar has been successful in achieving the lesser goal, whereas Antony, unsuccessful in the lesser, has been freed to achieve the greater.

Question 10.

Does Cleopatra remain the same throughout the play? Discuss.

Answer

There is in Cleopatra a development which parallels the development in Antony. It is less obvious, though. In the beginning of the play she is little more than an infinitely charming and regal woman who has the power to enslave men. She is devoted to Antony, but her expression of it is through her physical charms and her wit. She is given to play acting. It is a large part of her repertoire of tricks to keep her man interested in her. It is frequently excercised for the mere pleasure of acting. Her intensity of personality is somewhat superficial. She is filled with a fear for her own safety, exposed most disastrously at the battle of Actium. Antony's criticisms of her are partly justified. In certain ways she does put herself first.

The events of the play, though, have a profound effect upon her. Her love of Antony grows enormously and deepens into something more than physical passion. Through this love she overcomes her fears and accepts death with dignity and self-assurance. The playacting that she puts on for Caesar in the last act is meant to put him off his guard so that she can carry out her plan to join Antony in death. It is no longer an example of her old egocentric fears. She still has her old skill at acting and she deceives Caesar of her real intentions. We know this because she has prepared for her death long before she learns that Caesar means to lead her home in triumph. She sees with true clarity the falseness of Caesar's success.

> See, Caesar! O, behold,
> How pomp is followed! Mine will now be yours;
> And should we shift estates, yours would be mine.
> . . . . .
> O Caesar, what a wounding shame is this,
> That thou vouchsafing here to visit me,
> Doing the honor of thy lordliness
> To one so meek, that mine own servant should

Parcel the sum of my disgraces by
Addition of his envy! (Act V, Sc. 2, lines 183-199)

The mighty Caesar has succeeded in turning one of Cleopatra's servants against her. What honor is the achievement of power if it corrupts loyalty? Later, when she calls Charmian to bring her her "best attires", she puts them on in a different spirit than she did when she came to meet Antony the first time on her barge. Now she wears them so that he will recognize her when they meet in the after-world. They are the symbol of her queenliness of spirit; her crown is the symbol of her triumph over herself. When she dies and knocks this crown askew, Charmian pauses before her own death to set it straight. Cleopatra's death is an assertion of the spirit and the imagination over material things. In this achievement she is the greatest female figure that Shakespeare ever created.

Meaning

Methods of Analyzing Meaning

The meaning of a work of art is an exceptionally difficult thing to define. It is not the same thing as the plot or the central theme, but these quantities need to be understood before the meaning can be given. It may be approached by analyzing the individual meanings of the several aspects of the total play. When, for instance, we ask what the meaning of a symbol is, one answer might be that it is equivalent to the intellectual conception that stands behind the symbol, which is better conveyed if it is pointed at rather than explained. The value of a symbol over mere words is that it calls up emotional responses in the perceiver in some unconscious way which a longer and more detailed explanation would do less successfully. There are many layers of meaning in a rich symbol, as there are many levels of meaning in a Shakespearean play.

In *Antony and Cleopatra* the student should understand at least two levels of meaning. There is the obvious one that relates directly to the characters and situations of the play itself. This is clear when we understand the whys and wherefores of the behavior of the characters. Then there is a deeper level in which the author says something of significance about the human condition. We say this is deeper because it relates to something common to all people and not just to the play's characters. Until we know at least these two levels of meaning it is impossible to evaluate the work. In judging the worth of something it must be remembered that the criteria of worth vary in different historical and ethical periods of man's existence. An awareness of this subjectivity of judgment should keep the student from making absolute statements about the value of a work of art. The meaning as contrasted with the value of the meaning, however, is more accessible to a definite expression. The final statement of the meaning of the play will be the summation of a series of intellectual and emotional investigations. A good place to begin these is with the theme of the play.

1. Explaining the Theme

The theme of a piece of literature is the abstract thought or idea which the author wants to present before his audience. It is always of importance to him and he tries to make it be important to us, his readers. Frequently there is more than one theme, but usually these other themes are closely related to some central one. A work without any theme whatsoever is extremely rare and not likely to hold our interest for long. Most plays are the expression in action of an idea in the mind of the author. In writing he invents characters and situations which embody this theme and present it in a way that his readers can relate to easily. Our purpose is to apprehend the idea behind the actions and to translate it back into the abstract again. The organization of the material of the play, its division into acts and scenes, begins with the theme and is meant to show the stages in the development of the theme or themes. The concept of theme is one way of distinguishing fiction from real life. Real life is too random and unorganized to have a central theme; fiction is more limited in that it chooses a certain aspect of existence to concentrate on.

2. Relationship of Theme to Characters

The characters of a play embody the play's theme to the extent that they present in action what the theme says in words. Their doing this makes the theme seem more vital and real. One of the themes of *Antony and Cleopatra* is the emptiness of the quest for power when placed alongside the experience of love. Octavius Caesar illustrates the quest for power and is opposed by Antony who chooses love over power. Their struggle against each other brings out the meaning that love is the greater and more human. The situations give the characters room in which to demonstrate in action that the proposition of the theme is true.

3. Relationship of Plot to Meaning

The plot of a play may be defined very simply as what happens to the characters. The playwright begins the action with a given situation and particular characters. As the play unfolds these situations go in a certain direction, partly at the determination of the characters and partly so as to affect them. The meaning of the play as it is related to plot is contained in the explanation of why the given situation goes in the direction it does. A clear understanding of this will give an understanding of what the author is trying to say, what his meaning is.

4. Logic

After our analysis of the meaning of the play we must determine by the application of logic whether we are right about it. If we have perceived the meaning correctly then the actions of the characters will all seem logical; we will understand easily many of the small details of their behavior and of why the situations develop as they do. If we try to do this and cannot it is probably because our meaning is too narrow or not accurate. It may be, also, that the playwright has not been skillful enough or has been confused himself about what he means to say. This, however, is rarely the case with Shakespeare.

Questions and Answers on the Meaning of *Antony and Cleopatra*

Question 11.

What is the basic theme of *Antony and Cleopatra*?

Answer

Whenever there is an important conflict in a play it is certain that the theme of the play is closely related to this conflict. This is so in that the conflict works out of the theme in action. The conflict in *Antony and Cleopatra* centers around a choice that Antony faces and has to resolve. He has to choose between the world of power and dominion over men in which he is already recognized as the greatest soldier alive and that which is newer to him, the world of love and imagination. The choice is especially difficult because his entire present state of honor and respect derives from his success at war and power politics. This is all he has known until he comes to Egypt and Cleopatra. His behavior during the course of the play demonstrates that he is not yet at home with the new experience of passion and love. He has no external basis for making the choice, which has to come from within himself. The great glory for Antony is that he makes the deeper and more meaningful choice in a purely emotional way. He lets go of his drive to reassert his influence as a world figure and chooses the more intimate role as Cleopatra's lover. When we recognize that this is also Shakespeare's choice we are near to understanding what the theme of the play is. What finally convinces us that Antony's choice is also Shakespeare's is the history of the figure Octavius Caesar. As he is portrayed to us he is a symbol for success in the power struggle. The questions which thus must be asked are: What sort of person is he? How does he compare with Antony?

Caesar is an eminently practical man who never allows personal feelings to interfere with his central ambition to defeat all contenders for Roman power. He uses his sister, whom he obviously cares a great deal about, as a pawn to keep Antony bound to him. This is Caesar's way of controlling Antony. Further, he has Lepidus, the third member of the Triumvirate, arrested on apparently false charges, and so removes him as well. He is very cold in his dealings with all people. He does not even trust his close lieutenants. In the last act, for instance, Proculeius is sent to lie to Cleopatra about Caesar's true intentions for her. Then, not trusting Proculeius, he sends another lieutenant, Gallus, to watch Proculeius. Our reaction to Caesar in such situations is to remain a cool observer who can say: "Yes, that is the way to behave if you want to rule, but how shoddy and ignoble to have to act thus." Taking the positive side of the

96

theme as Antony's choice and the negative side of the theme as Caesar's, it is obvious that Shakespeare is saying that love means more in this world than the quest for power. The theme then might be stated somewhat as follows: the measure of a man is in the choices he makes, and between the ideals of love and power there is only one meaningful choice — love. If we, too, accept this choice, then we must also accept the fact that Antony's weaknesses in the sphere of action matter little.

Question 12.

What is the philosophy of life expressed in the play? To what extent can we infer that it is Shakespeare's own philosophy?

Answer

The answer to this question is really an elaboration of the explanation given in the last question. The theme of the play is related to the philosophy in the same way that an abstract idea is related to the living reality. The characters of Antony and Cleopatra are made so attractive that all our emotional sympathy goes out to them. When we observe people such as Caesar and Pompey we remain aloof and merely watchers. We never enter into an understanding with them. This immediate attraction to the title characters ought to indicate something special about them. Shakespeare never deludes us emotionally; he never pulls a surprise on his audience. If he works hard to create a bond of sympathy with a character we can be sure that this attachment is genuine and that Shakespeare feels it as well. What we feel about Antony and Cleopatra is that there is something wonderful in their relationship. It lifts us out of the realm of the ordinary and transports us into the world of the spirit. Everything they do and say seems to have a magical attraction. We do not remember their individual words as much as we do those of *Hamlet* or *Macbeth*, but we remember the mood of the play, the ecstasy we experience in their presence. Now, if instead of being the observers, we were the lovers themselves, how unbelievable that would be. In this sense they become our ideal of mature lovers who have experienced the world and found most of its glories wanting. In their maturity they have turned away from the public pomp and ceremony towards the intimate and personal. In their heightened imagination, a product of their mutual love, they seem to transcend the limits and limitations of the world.

As early as Act I, Scene 1, we hear:

Cleopatra: I'll set a bourn how far to be beloved.
Antony: Then must thou needs find out new heaven,
new earth.   (lines 16-17)

When Cleopatra learns that Antony must leave her, her grief has no bounds:

Cleopatra: Help me away, dear Charmian! I shall fall.
It cannot be thus long; the sides of nature

Will not sustain it. (Act I, Sc. 3, lines 22-23)

Later in the same scene Cleopatra says to Antony of their lovemaking:

> Eternity was in our lips and eyes,
> Bliss in our brows' bent, none our parts so poor
> But was a race of heaven. (lines 48-50)

Antony, in Act IV, Scene 8 compares Cleopatra to time itself:

> O thou day o' the world. (lines 14-15)

And lastly, after Antony's death, Cleopatra makes him seem to dominate the entire earth:

> His legs bestrid the ocean: his reared arm
> Crested the world. His voice was propertied
> As all the tuned spheres, and that to friends....

(Act V, Sc. 2, lines 101-112)

Shakespeare apparently is saying that there is another power in the world than the power over men, which can transcend the limitations of the world. This is the power of the imagination which is most fully expressed in love. We encounter this same philosophical thought in numerous other Shakespearean works, most particularly in his last comedy, *The Tempest*. Here the power of words and imagination are capable of transforming the entire visible world. They are like magic. The figure of the magician, Prospero, is surely a very personal creation of Shakespeare, perhaps even Shakespeare himself. We meet this philosophy as early as *Romeo and Juliet* where the power of love is the only thing able to end a bloody feud that has raged for several generations. Thus, at the same time that we discover the central theme of *Antony and Cleopatra* in several other plays by Shakespeare we must conclude that it is a very personal statement of the author's own philosophy.

Question 13.

In what ways is this a play of action, and in what way is it "actionless"?

Answer

The question of action is really a question of plot. The events that make up the play constitute the plot. At stake is the political fate of the then known world. Octavius Caesar is contesting the leadership of this world with Mark Antony. The outcome of this contest is decided by two serious battles, both of which Antony loses. Furthermore, there are several other military struggles mentioned: the war started by Fulvia; Antony's battle and defeat of Pompey; and the struggle with the Parthians. All these create an atmosphere of action and movement. It would seem that the fate of the world was to be determined by these wars of power. There is also the very important figure of Octavius Caesar who

98

is a man of *par excellence*. We get a sense that the fury of action drives the characters on to further action. Messengers hurry back and forth between the various camps with demands and news. A large part of Antony's desire is devoted to turning away from the inaction of Egypt back again to what he thinks of as his natural role as a man of action in the Roman leadership. Honor and reputation are acquired through the actions a successful soldier takes. In all these ways *Antony and Cleopatra* seems to be very much a play of action.

There is another side to the picture, though, which does not accord with this idea of the play as being primarily one of action and movement. The most prominent feature of the play is its use of imaginative language. We are much more conscious of the near-perfection of the characters' speech than we are of any action they take. The principal development of the play's theme occurs in the minds and hearts of the characters, not in any significant action which they take. Most, if not all, of the struggles occur offstage and are related to the audience by some observer. This is hardly the essence of a play in action. For instance, *Hamlet*, in which there is a problem of action versus inaction, is finally resolved in a scene filled with a stage full of action. The final scene of that play contains no less than four deaths and a duel. In *Antony and Cleopatra*, though, there is no similar resolution of the central conflict in action. Cleopatra's death is almost purely verbal and of the spirit. It is her words that stir us. Her descriptions of her lover rarely deal with his success as a soldier; they are more concerned with the huge spirit of the man.

All the changes that take place are the result of a deeper perception of the values of life; they are produced in the mind through the agents of feeling and thought, rather than through an understanding that action brings. In fact, many of the scenes would seem static and dull were it not for the high level of interest aroused by the spoken poetry. No other play by Shakespeare quite has this characteristic. Even the language cannot be said to have much internal movement towards the projection of ideas. It has reached a degree of perfection that is almost motionless, but not quite.

One of Shakespeare's underlying ideas or themes is that there is an illusion that action brings important results. Antony and Cleopatra live without this illusion. They have no need for it. They have in each other all that they can possibly need and want. What illusion they do have is the illusion which accompanies all lovers, that the world belongs to them, that they can live without the world. In the character of Caesar, Shakespeare clearly shows the illusion of action as truly an illusion. Caesar believes that he has conquered something all-important in wresting the Roman Empire from Antony and Lepidus. But to Shakespeare this is a hollow conquest. It can never be the subject of high poetry and imagination in the same way that Antony and Cleopatra's love can be. It is interesting that in his only borrowing from the ancient classics of action, the Homeric poems, his attitude is one of bitter irony and satire on the value and the heroic nature of such epic action. This is the play *Troilus and Cressida*. Thus the only answer possible to the above question is that although *Antony and Cleopatra* is a stage drama and therefore assumes a good deal of action, the real heart of the play is in the spirit of man, which is outside of time and movement.

Question 14.

Is *Antony and Cleopatra* a tragedy? Discuss.

Answer

Ultimately all criticism of this play has to come to terms with the nature of the tragedy it presents, if indeed it does present a tragedy. In the Greek concept of tragedy, a man of high station struggles against an inevitable fate and is finally destroyed by that fate because he fails to see it until it is too late. This, at least, is what happens in *Oedipus Rex* by Sophocles. Frequently the hero dies as a result of this struggle. *Hamlet, Macbeth, Othello*, and probably *King Lear* are good examples of Shakespearean high tragedy which follow, at least approximately, this classical conception. In these plays the physical world is limited to a large degree: there is a deep concentration of the characters upon the events that happen to them.

In *Antony and Cleopatra*, however, there is a much greater expansiveness of the characters and the thoughts than in these other works. Antony and Cleopatra are very much aware of the world and its forces. They do not reject the world until it rejects them. So the tragedy must be of a different sort than the traditional type of drama. If we extend the concept of tragedy to include the idea that one may struggle against the reality of the limitations of the world and be defeated by them then *Antony and Cleopatra* can conceivably be classed as a tragedy. This reality that Antony has to deal with is the incompatibility between the lust for power and the desire for love and intimacy. The world just does not allow these two things in the same person.

It is doubtful whether Antony ever understands and accepts this condition of existence. What happens to him is that he is defeated in his attempts to be successful in the power struggle and is thus forced to make the decision about love on its own merits. His glory is that he chooses love instead of bitter cynicism of the type of *Timon of Athens*. The tragedy, then, belongs to life which does not allow of too complete a satisfaction of desire. Part of this tragedy embodies itself in the debasement that Antony experiences as a result of his defeat. He behaves in a thoroughly inexcusable way. He has Caesar's Messenger beaten to satisfy his own frustration. It is a demeaning action which it is difficult to forgive him for. No other tragic hero of Shakespeare's falls quite so low as Antony does at this moment. His frequent turnings against Cleopatra, the object of his passion, are also difficult to justify. His failure at Actium is obviously not her fault, but his own in following after her. But only King Lear rises as high as Antony does in his gesture to Enobarbus and in his acceptance of Cleopatra at the end. Antony seems to do it out of his transformed nature rather than because he has understood the crisis he has passed through. In this he differs from Lear. Thus *Antony and Cleopatra* is much less intellectual than other Shakespearean tragedies. It culminates in a transcendence of the tragic situation and in an acceptance of a world of spirit that lies beyond tragedy. From this point of view it is intensely moving.

Question 15.

What attitude do Antony and Cleopatra take towards death?

Answer

At the beginning there is a difference in the attitudes that Antony and Cleopatra have towards their own deaths. By the conclusion of the play they feel very much the same about it. Cleopatra is initially fearful for her person. Her flight at Actium can be understood only if it is her person that she fears is in danger. The play-acting with Caesar in the last scene also derives from this fear. It is what is left over from her previous attitude towards her own death. But now she is no longer afraid and just acts as if she were in order to hide from Caesar her real intention to die. This change has come about through the effect her love for Antony and his death has had on her. His example has shamed her by its dignity and sacrifice. Now she only wants to hasten her own end so she can rejoin him in the beyond where he waits impatiently for her. She embraces death. With Antony, whoever has been steeped in the Roman tradition of stoicism, death is never a fearful master. We learn at the time of his own suicide that he had considered the possibility of his own death sometime before he had had his servant, Eros, promise to aid him in it. He preferred death to an ignoble life. At the point of his death, though, the loss of worldly honor is no longer centrally important. He dies because Cleopatra has sent her servant to tell him that she had died. He kills himself for a double reason, neither part of which would be considered Roman. He dies in remorse for his accusations against Cleopatra which caused her death, and because he wants to hurry after her and ask forgiveness. It is to be a reunion in a better world, a world that accepts their vision of reality and its truth of the heart.

But there is something else quite peculiar about both their attitudes towards death. They sexualize it. They go to death as if it were a lover waiting for them with open arms. Antony will be a bridegroom and death his lover:

> But I will be
> A bridegroom in my death, and run into't
> As to a lover's bed. (Act IV, Sc. 14, lines 121-123)

Thus, he is also, unconsciously, equating death with Cleopatra who is very much responsible for his. The idea of embracing death is a very

101

old one in the history of mankind and must touch some very deeply buried part of him. Cleopatra, at her death, treats death in practically the same way:

> If thou and nature can so gently part,
> The stroke of death is as a lover's pinch,
> Which hurts, and is desired.   (Act V, Sc. 2, lines 351-353)

Her end is not as quick as Charmian's is and she has time to elaborate on this theme:

> Peace, peace!
> Dost though not see my baby at my breast,
> That sucks the nurse asleep?   (lines 369-371)

Here the sexualization of death personified in the asp goes even further than before. It is equated with the child that is the richest expression of the sexual urge. Their concept of death is not the reality of no sensation, but the transcendence of this world into a world of fire and air, a world of pure spirit, where they will meet again. Death becomes a joyful experience for them. It releases them from the world which can find no place for them. (The above theme is further developed in a book by Ernest Schanzer called *The Problem Plays of Shakespeare*.)

Question 16.

What is the meaning of the structural parallelism in the actions and speeches of *Antony and Cleopatra*?

Answer

In the book mentioned in the last question, Ernest Schanzer points out a most interesting and significant parallelism in the character behavior of the title characters. It is one which the student should investigate on his own beyond what is said here. Schanzer accumulates textual evidence to support something we have felt all along: the identity that exists between the two lovers. The answer to the above question is a good example of how the elucidation of structural details contributes to the understanding of the meaning of the drama.

Let us first make a small collection of examples illustrating this idea and then judge what its meaning must be. In the answer to Question 15 we have already indicated the parallelism in their attitudes towards death. They share a similar feeling about value of material success in the struggle for power:

> *Antony*: Kingdoms are clay; our dungy earth alike
>   Feeds beast as man.   (Act I, Sc. 1, lines 40-41)

> *Cleopatra*: 'Tis paltry to be Caesar:
>   Not being Fortune, he's but Fortune's knave,
>   A minister of her will;   (Act V, Sc. 2, lines 2-4)

Both threaten or actually do treat a servant to a whipping. In Act II, Scene 5 the Messenger from Rome who brings the news that Antony has married Octavia has to suffer this threat from Cleopatra. She does not carry it out because she is a woman and not given to action as much as to words. In Scene 13 of Act III, Antony actually does have the Messenger, Thidias, whipped. With Antony the action is an attempt, paltry indeed, to reassert his power against the victorious Caesar. What we notice is that Antony acts out what Cleopatra only fantasizes. Both endure the pangs of jealousy, Cleopatra when she learns of Antony's marriage to Octavia, and Antony when he comes upon Caesar's servant kissing her hand. This jealousy is revived later and given the form of a memory of her relationship to Julius Caesar, so intimately connected with Octavius Caesar, when the Messenger from Octavius is caught kissing her hand.

> *Antony*: I found you as a morsel cold upon
>   Dead Caesar's trencher. Nay, you were a fragment
>   Of Gnaeus Pompey's, besides what hotter hours,
>   Unregist'red in vulgar fame, you have
>   Luxuriously picked out: for I am sure,
>   Though you can guess what temperance should be,
>   You know not what it is.   (Act III, Sc. 13, lines 144-150)

In their individual uses of language they seem to have a common imagination, not infrequently applying the same comparisons and images to each other. Each treats the other's name as if it were a categorical term which defined an entire world of experience. To be an "Antony" is to have all the traits of magnanimity and honor, forcefulness and generosity that Cleopatra finds in her lover.

> *Philo*: Sir, sometimes when he is not Antony
>   He comes too short of that great property
>   Which still should go with Antony.
>   (Act I, Sc.1, lines 66-68)

> *Cleopatra*: O, my oblivion is a very Antony,
>   (Act I, Sc. 3, line 114)

> *Cleopatra*: ...I will betray
>   Tawny-finned fishes. My bended hook shall pierce
>   Their slimy jaws; and as I draw them up,
>   I'll think them every one an Antony,
>   And say, "Ah, ha! y'are caught!"
>   (Act II, Sc. 5, lines 14-18)

> *Cleopatra*: It is my birthday.
>   I had thought t' have held it poor; but since my lord
>   Is Antony again, I will be Cleopatra.
>   (Act III, Sc. 13, lines 224-226)

> *Cleopatra*: I dreamt there was an Emperor Antony —
>   O, such another sleep, that I might see
>   But such another man!   (Act V, Sc. 2, lines 93-95)

Antony most frequently refers to Cleopatra by the name of Egypt, thus equating her with all that Egypt symbolizes in the play: luxuriousness, devotion to love, richness and strangeness of experience. He also calls her his Queen. His cry after the defeat at Actium suggests the broader meaning of his calling Cleopatra Egypt:

> O, whither hast thou led me, Egypt? (Act III, Sc. 11, line 54)

His inner struggle is not only against Cleopatra but also against all that Egypt means in the way of human experience. At his lowest moments he has to ask himself where the road he is travelling on is taking him. Right now all seems worthless since he has lost his honor in fleeing after Cleopatra and losing the battle.

There are many other structural parallels that the student can discover for himself: there are words they both use, images that describe them in similar terms, comparisons in which they are equated with the same third thing. One hardly noticeable event makes this equation of the two lovers very obvious:

> *Enobarbus*: Hush! Here comes Antony.
>
> *Enter Cleopatra.*
>
> *Charmian*: Not he! the Queen. (Act I, Sc. 2, lines 81-82)

Enobarbus, who knows Antony better than any other man, mistakes Cleopatra's approach for the arrival of his master. This makes no sense if it lacks the deeper significance suggested above and throughout the play by the repeated parallels between Antony and Cleopatra.

What does all this signify, then, in terms of the theme and total meaning of the play? Clearly, it must indicate some sort of identification of the lovers with each other through the love they feel. This identity is so profound a part of their being that they think and feel alike. Their imaginations have united and they function as the two halves of one entity. It is not surprising then that the rest of the world accepts this identity. We find those around Antony using phrases that those around Cleopatra use. Only Caesar tries to destroy this union, but to want to destroy it implies that he too recognizes its existence. Since the physical world prohibits a permanent and total union of the two spirits, that union can only occur beyond this world in that other world to which death is the entranceway. As each dies he hurries towards his death with the expectation of being reunited with the other. We see a similar situation, but on a much less mature level of conception, in *Romeo and Juliet*, where everything is almost pure romance. The union in *Antony and Cleopatra* transcends this concept of romance in that it engages the entire spectrum of human possibilities in a philosophical statement about the values of the imagination. For Antony and Cleopatra, who have experienced all there is in this world, there remains only the task of returning to fire and air.

Style

Methods of Analyzing Style

This word refers to a whole group of qualities directly related to the language that the author chooses to express his thoughts in. There are many separate components in it which should be looked at individually, such as diction, imagery, figurative language, emphasis, abstractions, rhythm, differences between this author's works and those of another author, etc. All of these are fairly difficult to discuss and sometimes even difficult to perceive, but they are near to the heart of the work. Much of the greatest pleasure in drama and poetry, as well as in prose, derives from the author's style. In writing, Shakespeare has to make an almost infinite number of word and image choices which can either work together harmoniously or can jar one against the other. One other important thing about style is that it is very personal and reflects something intimate about the author. After reading several works by an author we come to recognize his style. Since the choice of words is the foundation of style, it is wise to begin the study of style with diction.

Diction

The choice of words that a writer makes to express his ideas and the characters' emotions is said to be his diction. If we compare several works by Shakespeare, we will find that the diction in each is likely to be particular to that play. In the history plays, such as *King Henry V*, the diction is appropriate to the themes of war and kingship. In his romances and comedies, such as *As You Like It*, the diction fits the laughter and brighter situations. And in the tragedies, such as *King Lear*, the diction expresses the philosophical ideas and approach to nature that is central to the play. We also speak of a poetic diction as opposed to a prose diction. Shakespeare employs both in *Antony and Cleopatra*, and the student should notice when he uses each, and who uses which diction.

Imagery

An image is one form of a figure of speech. As its name implies it is a kind of picture of something in words which creates in us a feeling that straight descriptive words could not. The function of imagery, in addition to increasing the pleasure we take in the writing, is to develop more fully what is said or described by connecting it up with other aspects of the world from which the images are drawn. In *Macbeth*, as an example, there is a good deal of descriptive language, imagery, connected with the theme of light and dark. It is so prominent a feature of that play that we quickly realize that the problem of light and dark in the human soul is a central theme of the play. In *Antony and Cleopatra*, the imagery is concerned with the themes of love, honor, strange animals, the sun and the moon, death, etc. Taken all together these images point the attention to the themes themselves.

Figurative Language

Figurative language is the use the author makes of figures of speech such as similes, metaphors, analogies, personifications, hyperboles, antitheses, etc. It is these features of style that give the works of an author his personal stamp. It is by these that we know Shakespeare from Marlow or Ben Jonson. The author makes his choices out of his own experiences in life, physical and imaginative. The most frequently employed figures of speech are simile and metaphor and they are easy to identify. In a simile one object is said to be like another. In the very first speech in Antony and Cleopatra we have the following simile:

> *Philo:* Those his goodly eyes
> That o'er the files and musters of the war
> Have glowed like plated Mars...   (Act I, Sc.1, lines 2-4)

Here the eyes or glance of Antony is compared with that of the god Mars. In a metaphor one subject is said to be another, rather than merely like another. The essence of metaphor, then, is the identity between the two. The same speech contains also a good example of a metaphor.

> His captain's heart,
> ...is become the bellows and the fan
> To cool a gypsy's lust.   (lines 6-10)

The two parts of the simile or the metaphor may be separated from each other by intervening words, so care must be taken to discover it. This metaphor suggests many other meanings or levels of meaning than the obvious one that Antony's love is used by Cleopatra to satisfy her desire. It is the multiplicity of meanings that makes figurative language so rich.

Emphasis

Stylistically, the principle of emphasis is important because if the author follows it we are able to recognize which are the major themes and which the subsidiary ones. The idea is that the author devotes the most time, the most language, the greatest care, to that aspect of the meaning which he considers the most important. Our own sense of the way things should be will convince us that this is only proper. The rest of the work may be considered as detail which either adds to or elaborates the main center of emphasis. This is not only true of the style but of the structure as well. The point or points of emphasis are usually made clear by a heightening of the diction, and of the metaphors and imagery. In *Antony and Cleopatra* the emphasis is obviously on the relationship between the two lovers and how this comes into conflict with Antony's wish to restore his reputation to the level it was at before he came to Egypt. All the magnificent language of the play is saved for these moments. There is a decided falling off of beauty and interest in the language itself in those scenes involving Caesar and Pompey. Style, then, draws our attention to what is most important. The student must learn to notice this fluctuation in the various elements of the style and the structure. He must grow sensitive to stylistic differences that correspond to different settings (Rome vs. Egypt) and different types of character (Antony's vs. Caesar's; royalty's vs. slave's). With this in mind he can proceed to make other, more important, judgments based upon stylistic differences, such as the one that follows.

Point of View

There are two aspects to the question of point of view. One relates to the point of view of the individual work at hand, which may or may not correspond with the author's personal views. And the other relates to the more personal viewpoint which is the author's own. For instance, the author may be writing about war from the point of view of the victor, expressing the sentiments appropriate to that side. At the same time, he may himself feel the terrible futility of all war and be somewhat uncertain of the advantages accruing to the victor. Stylistic and structural emphasis will show us where the point of view of the play lies, but it takes the play as a totality to tell us the author's own viewpoint. In respect to most of Shakespeare's writing there a considerable critical disagreement about these matters. Thus, it is ultimately left to each student to make his own judgment of where the author places the important emphasis, and if this point of view differs from the author's own.

Subjective Elements of Style

It is worthwhile making the observation that the style of the author is very subjective, that is, that it derives from something inside his own being and not from something that can be measured by the scientist. The greatness of Shakespeare is closely connected with this element of subjectivity of style. As difficult as his language may seem to the student at times, Shakespeare is able to reach millions of people and convince them of the correctness of his point of view. In psychological terms we would say that he is in contact with the innermost strata of our common humanity and is able to show it to us. In addition to this, he also has personal convictions which many of his audience will not agree with. Some of these are attitudes which he holds only for the present moment and about which he felt differently in other periods of his life. This takes us to the last element of style to be mentioned.

Comparing to Style of Other Works by Same Author

If we undertake to compare the style of *Antony and Cleopatra* with the style of other plays by Shakespeare we should arrive at an understanding of what is unique about this play. The style of *Othello* is described as musical; that of *King Henry V* is military and royal; that of *Hamlet* intellectual. What, then, is the style of the present play? We will leave this to the student to define for himself.

Questions and Answers on the Style
of *Antony and Cleopatra*

Question 17.

How are the worlds of Rome and Egypt differentiated through the style of language?

Answer

The distinctness of the two worlds of Rome and Egypt is essential to the meaning of the play. They represent two significantly different attitudes to life. The difference between them is carried into the style of the language that the characters in Rome and Egypt speak in. By their speech alone we could tell the difference between Cleopatra and Octavia, between Antony and Caesar. As an example let us take a characteristic passage by each woman and see the differences. Both selections express a deep feeling.

> *Cleopatra*: Ah, dear, if I be so,
> From my cold heart let heaven engender hail,
> And poison it in the source, and the first stone
> Drop in my neck; as it determines, so
> Dissolve my life! The next Caesarion smite!
> Till by degrees the memory of my womb,
> Together with my brave Egyptians all,
> By the discandying of this pelleted storm,
> Lie graveless, till the flies and gnats of Nile
> Have buried them for prey!   (Act III, Sc. 13, lines 194-203)

> *Octavia*: O, my good lord,
> Believe not all; or if you must believe,
> Stomach not all. A more unhappy lady,
> If this division chance, ne'er stood between,
> Praying for both parts.
> The good gods will mock me presently
> When I shall pray "O, bless my lord and husband!"
> Undo that prayer by crying out as loud
> "O, bless my brother!" Husband win, win brother,
> Prays, and destroys the prayer; no midway
> 'Twixt these extremes at all.   (Act III, Sc. 4, lines 11-21)

In the first, Cleopatra is at pains to convince Antony that she is not coldhearted towards him. Her entire happiness is at stake. In the second, Octavia pleads to her husband, Antony, not to make war with her brother, Caesar, because this will cause her the pain of a divided loyalty. The first thing to notice is the richness of Cleopatra's diction, almost to the point of excess and the figurative paucity of Octavia's diction. Cleopatra repeats no important image word, but elaborates her feeling in a greatly extended metaphor. Octavia, on the other hand, repeats many of her words, particularly the word pray or prayer. Cleopatra, in a similar circumstance, would have been at pains to vary her expression. Octavia's language is sparse and to the point. Cleopatra revels in the love of words for themselves, at the same time that she uses them to heighten the emotion she feels. Her images are taken from the world of nature over which they wander from the animate to the inanimate. She mentions heaven, hail, stone, womb, storm, graves, flies, gnats, and the Nile. All that Octavia brings into her language are the gods to whom she appeals. Cleopatra is perfectly at home in the world of the spirit; Octavia is in awe of it and feels the necessity to propitiate it as if it were hostile. This difference in relationship to the world is a product of the mental environments they exist in. The long five-syllable pause in the fifth line of Octavia's speech contrasts sharply with the overflowing lines of Cleopatra's. It is obvious that Octavia would prefer not to have to verbalize her feeling, while it is easy for Cleopatra to expose her emotions.

Let us once more compare the speech of Egypt with that of Rome, this time contrasting Antony with Caesar.

Antony: I will be treble-sinewed, hearted, breathed,
         And fight maliciously. For when mine hours
         Were nice and lucky, men did ransom lives
         Of me for jests; but now I'll set my teeth
         And send to darkness all that stop me. Come,
         Let's have one other gaudy night. Call to me
         All my sad captains; fill our bowls once more.
         Let's mock the midnight bell.   (Act III, Sc. 13, lines 216-223)

Caesar: Take up her bed,
         And bear her women from the monument.
         She shall be buried by her Antony.
         No grave upon the earth shall clip in it
         A pair so famous. High events as these
         Strike those that make them; and their story is
         No less in pity than his glory which
         Brought them to be lamented.   (Act V, Sc. 2, lines 434-441)

The feeling of sadness pervades Antony's words. His reaction to the recent defeat at Actium is not directly expressed, but it is there in the language nevertheless. He resolves to be stronger-minded in the next encounter, and to fill up the time until then with pleasure. His thoughts recall his past glory and then turn away from such thoughts with his call for revelry. We are struck by the tension in the lines which correspond with the conflict in Antony. One should point out how many of the nouns and verbs are modified by adjectives and adverbs. When we examine Caesar's speech made at the end of the play, the difference is as obvious as that between Cleopatra and Octavia. His tribute to the two lovers is very unemotional; it is impossible to tell how much he really does feel about their deaths. He seems to be carrying out the required formalities without understanding the tragedy or the glory of this magnificent pair. The structure of the language is very barren of imagery. Only one noun is modified and even that rather coldly.

Further studies by the student along the lines suggested above will reveal more details in the stylistic differences between Rome and Egypt. Rome stands for a repression of emotions; Egypt for an open expression of them. Rome is a world given over to politics and quest for power; Egypt is a land of pleasure and enjoyment of living. Rome is single-minded in its view of life; Egypt is aware of the multifacetedness of human existence. The two places and the two philosophies they represent are as opposite as Shakespeare could make them.

Question 18.

Discuss the wit of the play as one aspect of the play's style.

Answer

The wit of the play is confined exclusively to those scenes in which either Antony or Cleopatra appear. We will define wit as that property of language which produces pleasure, and sometimes laughter, as a result of the enjoyment of what lies behind the words that express the wit. Thus, for example, there is considerable wit in the first exchange between Antony and Cleopatra.

> *Cleopatra*: If it be love indeed, tell me how much.
> *Antony*: There's beggary in the love that can be reckoned.
> *Cleopatra*: I'll set a bourn how far to be beloved.
> *Antony*: Then must thou needs find out new heaven,
> new earth. (Act I, Sc. 1, lines 14-17)

We feel at once that there is a contest going on between the two speakers, and that neither is the victor. Beyond this, the thought behind the words takes us immediately into the world of the play, into the larger world of the imagination, which does not suffer the same limitations as the physical world does. We enjoy the rapidity of the exchange. Each person speaks only one line at a time. This gives us a sense of confidence in the speakers that they are really in jest with each other and are in control of the situation. We also sense the expansiveness of the love bond between them which we only experience fully later. The imagination is entertained by the progress from "beggary" to "new heaven," including as it does the entire range of human experience. All these points about these mere four lines combine to delight the audience. This pleasure is the wit in the exchange.

In the early scenes of the play Cleopatra is given to play-acting in order to test Antony in the seriousness of his affection for her. The audience is perfectly aware that she is acting; it is as if we were let in on her secret and we can thus take pleasure in her success and in Antony's discomfort.

Charmian: Tempt him not so too far; I wish, forbear.
In time we hate that which we often fear.

Enter Antony.

But here comes Antony.

Cleopatra: I am sick and sullen.

Antony: I am sorry to give breathing to my purpose —

Cleopatra: Help me away, dear Charmian! I shall fall.
It cannot be thus long; the sides of nature
Will not sustain it.   (Act I, Sc. 3, lines 16-23)

Before Antony's entrance Cleopatra's apprehension warns her that he brings news dangerous to her happiness. Her object is to fend the news off and delay it. She uses the only device she knows, drawing attention to herself. It works, for Antony stops dead in the middle of his sentence as soon as he notices her in a near faint. But she does not actually have to faint: the mere suggestion of it has stopped Antony. The wit is in the pleasure we feel at her excellent success and in our position as knowledgeable observers. For the moment Antony is being duped, and because of the tremendous attractiveness of Cleopatra at this time we can enjoy his predicament. The wit turns serious when Antony presses his news on her in spite of her efforts. But by this time over forty lines of verse have passed. These are only two examples of Shakespeare's wit in *Antony and Cleopatra*. Other places where it is prominent are the scene on Pompey's galley where the dignified rulers of the world all get drunk and stupefied; Antony's description of the crocodile to Lepidus in Act II; Cleopatra's interview with the Clown who brings her the asp in the basket of figs; and a more bawdy humor in the scene where Charmian questions the Soothsayer about her fortune.

The wit of the play is an important element in the style because it is one of the ways in which Rome is differentiated from Egypt. At Rome all is deadly serious. Only matters of practical and immediate significance are discussed. In Egypt there is more time and interest in matters other than practical affairs, so much so that they interfere with the campaign against Caesar. Functionally, the wit is one of the ways in which Shakespeare obtains our sympathy for Cleopatra and Antony. If these two were as dry as Caesar, we might very well side with Caesar since he will obviously be the political victor and this success only becomes less attractive when it is compared with something more attractive. Thus, the wit acts as a point of emphasis among the many elements of the play which guides us towards the author's meaning. If we respond at all to the wit, we respond spontaneously, and spontaneity is of the soul of life. Here is a deeply subjective element. Why we should be immediately attracted by persons who are relaxed enough to be witty we do not know, but it is certain that most human beings are so attracted. The wit is thus, as indicative of a major difference between Rome and Egypt, able to bring us to empathize with Egypt with which it is associated. It is produced largely through words, and that it marks the emphasis of the drama's meaning becomes one of the elements of style.

Question 19.

What are some of the imagistic patterns in *Antony and Cleopatra*? How are these patterns able to enhance our understanding of the play?

Answer

The dominant imagistic pattern in *Antony and Cleopatra* is one connected with a conception of the vastness of the world and which finds innumerable images and metaphors to refer to this vastness. Caroline Spurgeon in her book *Shakespeare's Imagery* points out that the single most important word in the play is significantly the word "world," which occurs forty-two times. This emphasis on vastness is achieved by images that come from the science of Astronomy. There are references to the following heavenly phenomena: moon, sun, stars, day, night, seasons, clouds, rain, air, tides, and more. At the same time these are treated as nature images. Here are a few examples:

Antony: Then must thou needs find out new heaven, new earth   (Act I, Sc. 1, lines 16-17)

Antony: . . . our dungy earth alike/ Feeds beast as man.   (Act I, Sc. 1, lines 40-41)

Soothsayer: In nature's infinite book of secrecy/ A little I can read.   (Act I, Sc. 2, lines 10-11)

Enobarbus: They are greater storms and tempests than almanacs can report. This cannot be cunning in her; if it be, she makes a shower of rain as well as Jove.   (Act I, Sc. 2, lines 164-167)

Caesar: This common body,/ Like to a vagabond flag upon the stream,/ Goes to and back, lackeying the varying tide,/ To rot itself with motion.
(Act I, Sc. 4, lines 49-52)

Cleopatra: Think on me,/ That am with Phoebus' (the sun) amorous pinches black/ And wrinkled deep in time.   (Act I, Sc. 5, lines 32-34)

Antony: The April's in her eyes. It is love's spring,/ And these the showers to bring it on.
(Act III, Sc. 2, lines 53-54)

Antony: When my good stars that were my former guides/ Have empty left their orbs and shot their fires/ Into the abysm of hell.   (Act III, Sc. 13, lines 177-179)

Enobarbus: Now he'll outstare the lightning.
(Act III, Sc. 13, line 236)

Cleopatra: O sun/ Burn the great sphere thou movest in!

Darkling stand/ The varying shore o' the world.

(Act IV, Sc. 15, lines 12-13)

One immediately notices that except for the quotation by Caesar where he refers to the movement of the tide, all of the references come from persons connected with Egypt and its way of life, or connected with either Cleopatra or Antony. It is characteristic of this grouping of images that they belong to Egypt. This is another stylistic device by which Rome and Egypt are sharply differentiated. The world expands towards infinity in the minds and words of Antony and Cleopatra. They already know all there is to know about the earth, and it is too limited for their limitless imaginations.

Another imagistic pattern that likewise separates Rome from Egypt is the frequent use of names from classical mythology. All of those referred to are either men, or gods and goddesses of high dignity and honor. This list includes: Mars, Venus, Jupiter, Phoebus (Apollo), Bacchus, Mercury, Juno, Hercules, Hector, Ajax, Dido and Aeneas, and a number of others. Such a collection of mythological figures places the lovers themselves in the world of mythology and legend. Some of the other characters mentioned are related more specifically to the theme of sexuality: Nessus, Cupid, Narcissus. On the other side, the Roman side, there are very few imagistic patterns, but there is one valuable to point out. This is the large number of images relating to war and the past history of the Roman Empire.

Ventidius: Now, darting Parthia, art thou stroke, and
now pleased fortune does of Marcus Crassus'
death/ Make me revenger. (Act III, Sc. 1, lines 1-4)

The words "darting" and "stroke" partake of the aggressiveness of war. "Revenge" and "death" are the cause and result, respectively, of war.

Caesar: When thou once/ Wast beaten from Modena,
where thou slewest/ Hirtius and Pansa, consuls,
at thy heel/ Did famine follow, whom thou
foughtst against/ (Though daintily brought up)
with patience more/ Than savages could suffer.

(Act I, Sc. 4, lines 63-68)

Here again the main theme of the diction and imagery is war — "beaten," "slewest," "famine," "foughtst," "savages," and "suffer." There is a remarkable piling-up of these theme images, so that the effect is emotionally very pronounced.

Another collection of images worthwhile for the student to examine on his own is that of all the animals mentioned. There, too, the range will be found to extend from the smallest "gnat" and "fly" to the powerful "crocodile" and "lion." As with the question of wit, the groupings of images into patterns is an important aspect of the style by which Shakespeare regulates the emphasis of the drama. Image patterns require much more detailed study to discover them than does any other aspect of style. It is a very subtle feature and probably is worked out in the author's unconscious mind. He feels about his groupings of characters in certain ways and his thoughts follow his feelings in the choosing of the diction in a way that corresponds with his emotions, but without his being particularly conscious of the process of choosing. Our study of image patterns can help to convince us of the correctness of our judgments about the point of view of Shakespeare with respect to the meaning of the play. It also makes us more attentive to the subtleties of the work which, in turn, increases our pleasure.

Selected Criticisms

Antony and Cleopatra has had an oddly uneven history. It has meant many different things to different men through the years and produced a broad spectrum of values and interpretations. These readings can be grouped pretty generally into three categories; of course, these categories will often overlap. In rough chronological order the points of view from which critics have viewed the play are: (1) the moral; (2) the aesthetic; (3) the political.

Dryden

The first great commentator on Shakespeare's plays was the seventeenth century playwright and man of letters, John Dryden. He expressed his dissatisfaction with *Antony and Cleopatra* by writing a play of his own on the same story, mending what he thought were the flaws in Shakespeare's version. The title he gave his play shows immediately how he construed its theme: *All For Love*. And its subtitle is a commentary on what Antony has lost in order to pursue his tragic love for Cleopatra: or, *The World Well Lost*. He recasts the materials of Shakespeare's play so as to make sharper the clash between the Egyptian queen and the Roman Empire, between love and honor; and to make more dramatic Antony's tragic choice. Dryden and his time were chiefly concerned, as he says in his Preface, with "the excellency of the moral: For the chief persons represented were famous patterns of unlawful love; and their end accordingly was unfortunate." Dryden retells the tale so as to make clearer that Antony and Cleopatra are punished at the end for their crimes: "The crimes of love, which they both committed, were not occasioned by any necessity, or fatal ignorance, but were wholly voluntary; since our passions are, or ought to be, within our power." This moral interpretation of the play as the downfall or punishment of its guilty protagonists and the triumph of the Roman ideal of honor became a model for later critics.

Dryden was also dissatisfied with the form of Shakespeare's play. He felt its rambling looseness of construction not only obscured the moral theme but violated the rules of dramatic composition. These rules were known as the unities of action, place and time, and required that the story dramatized in a tragedy should be single and simple with no subplots, and that it all occur in the same place during a single day, or circuit of the sun. So Dryden made his play conform to these rules of dramatic composition because, for moral reasons, he conceived of it as a tragedy. About *All For Love*, he says, "The fabric of the play is regular enough . . . and the unities of time, place and action more exactly observed" than in Shakespeare's version.

Dryden's play was a great success and so conformed to the tastes and conventions of his time and later that it took the place of *Antony and Cleopatra* on the London stage until 1759. Since 1606/7 when it was first performed, there is no record of a major performance of Shakespeare's play until it was revived by David Garrick in 1759. It was promptly dropped again. Despite a lavish and expensive production and five months of preparation, the play "did not seem to give ye Audience any great pleasure or draw any applause." But it is clear that the interpretation of the play had changed. It was no longer the solemn moral tragedy as conceived by Dryden but a spectacular theatrical showpiece.

Johnson

This change is clearer in the brief notes of Samuel Johnson, inserted in his 1765 edition of the play. He believed that the play's "power of delighting is derived from the frequent changes of the scene . . ." The reason he stresses the spectacle — the hurry of the action and variety of incident — is that he conceives of the play not as a tragedy but as a history, or chronicle play. "The events, of which the principal are described according to history, are produced without any art of connection or care of disposition." So Shakespeare, he feels, was retelling the history of the period, not the tragic defeat of its title characters. Consequently, for him these characters diminish in importance: "No character is very strongly discriminated," he says. But though the conception of what Shakespeare was doing has changed, the old moral interpretation shows itself still in Johnson's comments when he speaks of "the feminine arts, some of which are too low, which distinguish Cleopatra . . ."

Coleridge

S.T. Coleridge continues this tradition in the early part of the nineteenth century, but in his *Notes on Shakespeare* the moral judgment is mellower and the opposition between chronicle and tragedy is less extreme. Cleopatra is still the model of unlawful passion, but now the passion is more pardonable. "The sense of criminality in her passion is lessened by our insight into its depth and energy, at the very moment that we cannot but perceive that the passion itself springs out of the habitual craving of a licentious nature . . ." Her love for Antony is guilty also in that it is not a natural or spontaneous emotion but one nurtured and supported by her own wiles and associations. Although he condemns their love as an unlawful one, Coleridge does not read their suffering and death as an ignominious punishment for it. But he does group the play with the great tragedies, and says that in "its strength and vigour of maturity" it rivals *Macbeth*, *Lear*, *Hamlet*, and *Othello*. It is this strength and vigor of the play's style which expresses the depth and energy of the hero's unlawful passion and which makes it pardonable, though still unlawful. Coleridge is the first to feel that the magnificent poetry of the play, its style, makes the immoral characters magnificent in their doom. He says of this style: *Feliciter Audax*, or "daring but successful." The style is daring because it tries to meld together two distinct forms: tragedy and history. It is successful because Shakespeare's close allegiance to his historical source does not weaken its dramatic structure. It is both history and tragedy at once. By means of its daring style, history comes alive: "numerous momentary flashes of nature" counteract "the historic abstraction." And to show that it demonstrates surpassing judgment as well as genius, Coleridge compares it to Dryden's more regular play.

Hazlitt

William Hazlitt, a contemporary of Coleridge, shares his admiration for the poetry of *Antony and Cleopatra*. "This is a very noble play," he says of it, but does not rank it in the first class of Shakespeare's plays as Coleridge does. Hazlitt points out particularly how well the leading characters are realized: they "breathe, move and live." And Cleopatra is the masterpiece among them. Her "whole character is the triumph of the voluptuous, of the love of pleasure and the power of giving it, over every other consideration." He describes the variety with which Shakespeare has endowed her. "She is voluptuous, ostentatious, conscious, boastful of her charms, haughty, tyrannical, fickle. The luxurious pomp and gorgeous extravagance of the Egyptian queen are displayed in all their force and lustre, as well as the irregular grandeur of the soul of Mark Antony." We sense here the note of moral censure rising in the burden of his praise. The note grows louder when he says "Antony's headstrong presumption and infatuated determination to yield to Cleopatra's wishes to fight by sea instead of land, meet a merited punishment . . ." But whatever their vices, the virtues of the poetic style gloss them over. We admire these weak or flawed characters because of the poetry they speak. It is this poetic conception of character which is able "partly perhaps to place the effeminate character of Mark Antony in a more favourable light . . ." Like Antony, Cleopatra "had great and unpardonable faults, but the grandeur of her death *almost* redeems them. She learns from the depth of despair the strength of her affection." But only "almost."

Hazlitt does not read the play as a strict tragedy because it conforms to known facts. He calls it rather Shakespeare's finest historical play: "He made poetry the organ of history." But the history is so reshaped by the poetry as to bring out its latent significances. And so, simple chronicle becomes a contest between Roman pride and Eastern magnificence. This epic quality of its dimensions, he judges, derives from its disregard of the dramatic unities of time and place.

Later Criticism

The late nineteenth century critic A.C. Bradley echoes much of what Coleridge and Hazlitt have observed. He speaks of "the immense scale and world-wide issue of the conflict," i.e., its epic proportions. This epic quality makes itself felt in other ways: in the absence of dramatic action or dramatization of historical fact in Act I to III; in the defectively loose construction of Acts III and IV. The outward conflict of the play is the political struggle for power; we turn for relief from it to the real center of the drama, the fate of the lovers who are sure to lose it. The contrast between these two dramas, venal politics and tragic love, has two results: first, it blunts our feeling of the greatness of Antony's fall from prosperity; second, it emphasizes the positive element in the final tragic impression, the element of reconciliation.

But Bradley does not group this play with Shakespeare's four great tragedies, because it fails to produce the overwhelming tragic effect. The moral judgment of the play is too much softened by an admiration and sympathy for the lovers for us to condemn their love entirely; yet that love is too destructive for us to applaud it. We cannot rejoice to see them destroyed; but we know it must be so. "It is plain that the love of Antony and Cleopatra is destructive; that in some way it clashes with the nature of things; that while they are sitting in their paradise like gods, its walls move inward and crush them at last to death. This is no invention of the moralizing critics . . . But then to forget because of it the other side, to deny the name of love to this ruinous passion, to speak as though the lovers had utterly missed the good of life, is to mutilate the tragedy and to ignore a great part of its effect upon us. For we sympathise with them in their passion." But our pity ought not blind our moral judgment. "With all our admiration and sympathy for the lovers, we do not wish them to gain the world. It is better for the world's sake, and not less for their own, that they should fail and die." The softening or romanticizing of the moral judgment has gone quite far since Dryden rewrote the play as a conflict of unlawful love and honor. And along with this change in the play's meaning has gone a revision of the moral calibre of the characters, especially Cleopatra. She has been transformed by this critical trend from a whore — a pattern of unlawful love — to a constant and noble lover. Bradley believes that in Act V "she becomes unquestionably a tragic character, but, it appears to me, not till then." And he finds "what raises Cleopatra at last into pure tragedy is, in part, that which some critics have denied her, her love for Antony."

Twentieth Century Criticism

Thus by the start of the twentieth century the critical lines are

117

drawn. There are two general interpretations of the play which correspond to the two views, Egyptian and Roman, expressed in the play. The moralist school adopts the Roman view that Antony's love is mere dotage, infatuation, his downfall the ignoble effect of debauchery. They stress his growing folly and his cruelty. Cleopatra becomes simply a harlot to their eyes; a very successful, even a great, one, but still a harlot. Her death, like his, is a just and inevitable end. Their method is historical. Because of the growing romanticism, this school goes back to Shakespeare's own times for evidence to establish its case. The aesthetic school develops the Egyptian point of view. These critics acknowledge much of the moral censure of their colleagues, but try to show that the usually severe condemnation of such love and of the lovers' actions generally, are softened and even overcome by the magnificent poetry which they speak. The final scenes of the play, they maintain, are a hymn of praise to the nobility of love's sacrifice. Though the lovers die, no moral censure is possible. In fact we sympathize with them completely at the end. A third school of critics, using the same historical method as the moralists, tries to escape the dilemma by interpreting the play from neither the moral nor the aesthetic but the political point of view. They are closer in their discussions to the former group than to the latter.

The Moralist Schools

The greatest of those to speak against anachronistic criticism and to emphasize the theatrical virtues of the play as originally staged is Harley Granville-Barker. His *Preface* is still a classic piece of theatrical direction and criticism. He feels that "a larger theme than the love-story is being worked out" in the spacious field of world politics. Their balance has been lost, he says, by arbitrary division of the play's continuous action into act and scenes. These two themes are abreast — "Antony's concord with Caesar seen in the wane while, Cleopatra, spiderlike, sits spinning a new web for him . . ." However, Barker's preoccupation with theatrical effects leads him away from an interpretation which depends upon poetic effects derived from a close study of the imagery. Antony dies as he has lived, "a soldier and a sportsman — and a gentleman by his lights — to the end." He greets his death stoically: "Shakespeare spares him no ignominy; yet out of it rises . . . a man set free of debt to fate . . ." Barker does not try to resolve the contradictions or inconsistencies in Cleopatra's character by making her either harlot or saint. The effort of the actress must be rather to maintain the antitheses in her disposition and her infinite variety. "From wantonness, trickery and folly, Shakespeare means to lift her to a noble end. But, even in doing it, he shirks no jot of the truth about her." And her final resignation, even joyful acceptance of death, is the "failure's contempt for success." Her death is not "high spiritual tragedy." She dies "defiant, noble in her kind, shaming convenient righteousness, a miracle of nature that — here is the tragedy — will not be reconciled to any gospel but its own."

E.K. Chambers

Another of the moralist critics is E.K. Chambers, who did so much in the history of the Elizabethan theatre. Of Antony he says, "the instinct of domination and the instinct of sex are at odds in him; and if he chooses the worse course it is not without clear consciousness on his part of the issues at stake." Of Cleopatra, that she "is so conceived that she is fit to mate with her lover" because "love that is to be the scourge of the world, even if it is rooted in sensuality, must possess the attributes of majesty." "She is half courtesan and half a grande amoureuse." Their hypnotic love is "baleful" but so intense as to make it "worthy" of the tragedy. Of the play itself he concludes that in it, "Honor of chivalry and love of women . . . must stand their arraignment . . . Shakespeare returns to the double theme to strip the mask of worship from the spectre of agoism, and to indict passion as the ruin of greatness . . ."

Other Critics

More recent rebels against canonization of Antony and Cleopatra are John F. Danby, L.C. Knights, Franklin M. Dickey and Willard Farnham. Danby sees in the play opposites juxtaposed, mingled and married: "Then from the very union which seems to promise strength, dissolution flows." This polarity of opposites he calls "the World," represented by Caesar and Rome, and "the Flesh," represented by Cleopatra and Egypt. Antony must choose between them; but because neither would exhaust his potential, either would prove his downfall. So Shakespeare, he concludes, is not censuring either, but both, the very choice that limits itself. Antony and Cleopatra are both strumpet and fool *and* love's champions; or rather the play as a whole is Shakespeare's statement that such judgment may not be made.

L.C. Knights applauds Danby's conclusion, blames the romantic fallacy on the misinterpretation of Cleopatra's final speech as the *total* meaning of the play rather than merely one part of it. Antony's passion he describes as self-centered, self-consuming, especially after the battle of Actium: "At the superb close, Cleopatra — both empress and lass unparalleled — is an incarnation of sexual passion, of those primeval energies that are both necessary and destructive, that insistently demand fulfillment in their own terms, and, by insisting on their own terms, thwart the fulfillment that they seek."

Dickey's researches into cultural and literary history lead him to conclude, on the bases of classical and medieval authorities, and Elizabethan moral philosophy, that "Cleopatra appears again and again as wanton and a sorceress, who employed all the conscious arts of love to keep Antony ensnared." The Elizabethan spectator, he claims, "instead of seeing Antony and Cleopatra as patterns of nobility and of deathless love . . . must have seen them as patterns of lust, of cruelty, of prodigality, of drunkenness, of vanity, and, in the end, of despair."

Willard Farnham's comments directly oppose him to Bradley. He finds the play not a drama of their love but of Antony's rise and fall in the struggle for world power *after* he meets Cleopatra. Shakespeare "does not show the world to be, to the losers, as nothing compared to their love." That love, "like themselves, never ceases to be deeply flawed, however much it becomes capable of arousing admiration." He rejects the romantic or "Egyptian" view because "it was not the tendency of the age in which Shakespeare wrote to wash out the faults of Antony and Cleopatra in romantic sentiment . . . Nor can it be said with truth that the final effect of Shakespeare's play is a romantic washing out of the faults of his hero and heroine." His sympathy for them does not save them from his moral judgment. Their downfall and suffering in this last of the tragedies are not the instruments of a mysterious and capricious destiny but the inexorable working out of a flaw in character.

Aesthetic School

The aesthetic school of interpretation, which corresponds to the Egyptian point of view, is anticipated by an early historical critic whose study of the relation between the play and its sources is still standard. M.W. MacCallum rejects the moralist view of alternatives: "If (their) love were not mutual, Antony would be merely the toy of the courtesan, Cleopatra merely the toy of the sensualist. But in point of fact, it is mutual and sincere." And like the later romanticizers, he feels that in the final scenes, "their oneness of heart and feeling is indeed...complete, and their love is transfigured" by the beauty and nobility of the poetry.

The aesthetic school really flourished in the 1930's with an increased interest in Shakespeare's plays as poetry rather than theatre. Caroline Spurgeon reads the play primarily for its imagery and discovers a number of thematic images which establish the background or atmosphere of the play. Chief among these is "the world," mentioned forty-two times, and always giving the impression of "the expanse of the world and the tremendous consciousness of power on the part of the characters." The "imperial theme" is established by references to the grandeur of empire. Mark Van Doren later elaborated on both these themes in his interpretation of the play. Another image which provides tone for the play is "the Herculean hero," the giantlike dimensions of Antony and Cleopatra, which also provides Eugene M. Waith with the material for his study. W.H. Clemen, a German critic, expands the method and conclusions of Spurgeon. Besides creating atmosphere, the imagery "is symbolically related to the characters, serves their self-interpretations and the expression of their feelings." He is not troubled by the ambiguity of Cleopatra's character. "She is neither solely queen, nor solely harlot, nor solely witch, but unites in her person all these contrasting natures."

G.K. Knight

An extreme example of the aesthetic school is G.W. Knight. A close

120

student of the imagery of the play, he draws from it large philosophical conclusions as to Shakespeare's meaning. He finds in Cleopatra a metaphysical, not moral, good — a good of *totality*. She is good in the same large way one might say life is good, or the universe is good, not because it contains no suffering or bad times, but because from retrospect even these experiences are worth having. Cleopatra is a personification blend of good and evil; her "perfection flowers from totality, not exclusion." "Out of her varying moods, passions, experiences, one fact emerges: her serene love of Antony." The audience shares this transcendence of moral questions in the beauty of the poetry. "We watch as though from turrets of infinity, whence the ethical is found unreal and beauty alone survives." And of the characters he concludes, "In no play is the moral outlook so irrelevant as a means to distinguish the persons: it is rather an impossibility, has no meaning."

G.B. Shaw and D.A. Traversi

After Knight, much of the criticism of this school seems bent on proving G.B. Shaw's analysis of the play correct. In the Preface to his *Plays for Puritans*, Shaw says, with perhaps more than wind in his cheek, that "After giving a faithful picture of the soldier broken down by debauchery, and the typical wanton in whose arms such men perish, Shakespeare finally strains all his huge command of rhetoric and stage pathos to give a theatrical sublimity to the wretched end of the business, and to persuade foolish spectators that the world was well lost by the twain." D.A. Traversi would agree with much of this, with this proviso: that Shakespeare's "rhetoric" is poetry; his "pathos," tragic suffering; the "sublimity," real; the "strain," successful; the folly, wisdom. He certainly recognizes (as does Knight for that matter) the sordid realism of the play. "Antony's love is justified in terms of its intensity and vitality *in spite* of his continual awareness that Cleopatra is "a whore of Egypt" . . . in spite of the fact that his passion is the infatuation of a middle-aged soldier for a woman who had already served Julius Caesar's pleasure." Shakespeare, he admits, never disguises either Antony's incompetence or Cleopatra's corruption. But he believes both their venality and their stupidity are overcome by the brilliance of the poetry, the "poetic redemption," so to speak, of their love. Antony's "mad renunciation of practical affairs is balanced by the splendid assertion of his love," and Cleopatra's corruption becomes the fertile decay which breeds new life. So at the end "Antony's suicide becomes an integral part of the final lyrical assertion of the value and transcendence of passion. It looks forward to the poetry of Cleopatra's death . . ." This welding of opposites in the play, incompetence with wisdom, promiscuity with love, sordid realism with the most exalted poetry, leads Traversi to conclude that *Antony and Cleopatra* is "the play in which Shakespeare came nearest to unifying his experience into a harmonious and related whole."

Maurice Charney

The latest and most extended statement of the aesthetic viewpoint is by Maurice Charney; it is also the soberest and most measured statement. He believes that neither Roman nor Egyptian viewpoint is wholly correct; the very positioning of alternatives is wrong. "It is necessary," he says, "to hold both the Egyptian and Roman themes in the play together in the mind as a tragic unity. Either without the other makes for distortion and incompleteness. Taken alone, the Roman point of view simplifies the tragedy into a morality play, and the Egyptian one transforms the tragedy into a poem of transcendental love." It is impossible to hold one set of values as right and the other as wrong. "There is a quality of "somber realism" here that is neither moralistic nor rhapsodic, and the tragic conflict is not conceived as an alternation between Love and Honor." And he concludes, "The tragic choices of this play are between different kinds of rightness."

Charney finds two distinct tragedies in the play. Antony's is largely political. And so with his death "rather than being resolved, the conflict between Egypt and Rome ceases to exist . . . dissolved into an ecstatic poetic reality." This poetry of the lovers salvages their love and ennobles it. "Suicide is Cleopatra's tragic choice, and she is ennobled by it although she does not become a full-scale tragic protagonist as Antony does. Her tragedy is very clearly focused on this choice, whereas Antony is made to bear the burden of choice, responsibility, and guilt throughout the play. We may say, then, that Cleopatra begins as a temptress or enchantress rather than a tragic figure, but she is drawn up into tragedy by Antony's death." Whereas Farnham saw this as the last of Shakespeare's great tragedies, Charney sees it in certain respects as the first of his late romances.

The Political View

Avoiding these two alternatives, the moralist and the aesthetic, the political viewpoint gives greater weight to the world-power struggle in the play; Antony's downfall becomes political or military, Cleopatra just one more of his conquests. Lord David Cecil, seeing the play as more panorama than drama, tries to explain its meaning in this way. He believes that the great variety of mood, the vast distances covered, the swiftly changing scenes, the absence of unity, pattern, or dramatic significance, stem from Shakespeare's historical attitude to his subject. He is retelling history, not creating drama. However, the play does achieve a unity and a significance of sorts, and this he believes is due to Shakespeare's single presiding theme. "This theme is not love; it is success." The real conflict of the play is "the chaotic spectacle of the great world convulsed in the struggle for power and happiness . . ." And so he concludes, "The real test is between Antony and Octavius." Of the lovers, he says, "Antony's love is a self-indulgent passion that weakens his will and blinds his judgment. While Cleopatra is, by a strict moral

122

standard, a vain, worthless, capricious coquette . . ." Yet they are transformed, he feels, by Shakespeare's mature poetic style. Shakespeare's "conclusion seems to be that it is impossible to be certain in our judgment of Antony's conduct." Thus he avoids either the moralist or the aesthetic point of view.

Another political critic is T.J.B. Spencer. He buttresses his position with historical scholarship. In Shakespeare's time, he tells us, "ancient, in particular, Roman history was used as the material for political lessons, because it was one of the few bodies of consistent and continuous historical material available." Because the audience was well acquainted and concerned with it, "When Shakespeare turned . . . to Roman history as the subject of plays, he was touching upon grave and provocative problems of political morality, already much discussed." So much for the audience; the play also reveals a political bias. Shakespeare's concentration on the two title characters "does not impair our impression of the imperial theme. Cleopatra . . . does not dominate the play. Her self-centered nature is even more apparent because the real subject of the play is conflict in Antony, who is repeatedly confronted with a choice between his love for Cleopatra and his loyalty to the political and moral dignity of Rome." Here the political comes rather close to the moral; Spencer also shares some of the attitudes of the aesthetic school. "The poetry of the play exalts love. The splendour of language given to Cleopatra and to Antony, captures our imaginative sympathy for the losing side, for the 'wrong side'." But despite the poetry it remains the 'wrong' side, because it lost.

Bibliography

ARMSTRONG, Edward A. *Shakespeare's Imagination*, University of Nebraska Press, 1963.

BRADLEY, A.C. *Shakespeare's Antony and Cleopatra* in *Oxford Lectures on Poetry*, London, 1950.

CASE, R.H. and RIDLEY, M.R. Introduction to the Arden edition of *Antony and Cleopatra*, Cambridge, Mass., 1955.

CHAMBERS, E.K. *Shakespeare: A Survey*, London, 1925.

CHARNEY, Maurice. *Shakespeare's Roman Plays*, Cambridge, Mass., 1961

COLERIDGE, S.T. *Notes and Lectures Upon Shakespeare*, London, 1849, V.I, 145-148.

COLIE, Rosalie L. "Antony and Cleopatra: The Significance of Style," in *Shakespeare's Living Art*, Princeton, 1974 .

DANBY, John F. *Poets on Fortune's Hill*, London, 1952.

DICKEY, Franklin M. *Not Wisely, But Too Well*, San Marino, Calif., 1957.

DOWDEN, Edward. *Shakespeare*, N.Y., 1881.

DRYDEN, John. Preface to *All For Love* in Mermaid Series, London, 1949-50.

FARNHAM, Willard. *Shakespeare's Tragic Frontier*, Berkeley, Calif., 1950.

GRANVILLE-BARKER, Harley. *Prefaces to Shakespeare*, Princeton, N.J., 1952, V.I.

HAZLITT, William. *Characters of Shakespeare's Plays*, London, 1957.

HOLZKNECHT, Karl J. *The Background of Shakespeare's Plays*, N.Y., 1950.

JOHNSON, Samuel. *Samuel Johnson on Shakespeare* (ed. W.K. Wimsatt, Jr.), N.Y., 1960.

KNIGHT, G. Wilson. *The Imperial Theme*, London, 1951.

KNIGHTS, Lionel C. *Some Shakespearean Themes*, Stanford, Calif., 1960.

MacCALLUM, M.W. *Shakespeare's Roman Plays*, London, 1910.

MACK, Maynard. Introduction to the Pelican edition of *Antony and Cleopatra*, Baltimore, 1960.

RABKIN, Norman. *Shakespeare and the Common Understanding*, New York, 1967.

RIBNER, Irving. *Patterns in Shakespearean Tragedy*, N.Y., 1960.

ROSEN, William. *Shakespeare and the Craft of Tragedy*, Cambridge, Mass., 1960.

SPENCER, T.J.B. *Shakespeare: The Roman Plays*, London, 1963.

SPURGEON, Caroline. *Shakespeare's Imagery*, Boston, 1958.

SYMONS, Arthur. "*Antony and Cleopatra*" in *Studies in the Elizabethan Drama*, London, 1920.

TRAVERSI, D.A. *Approach To Shakespeare*, London, 1938.

VAN DOREN, Mark. *Shakespeare*, N.Y., 1939.

WILSON, Harold S. *On The Design of Shakespearean Tragedy*, Toronto, 1957.